seven soulful secrets

seven soulful secrets

FOR FINDING YOUR PURPOSE AND

MINDING YOUR MISSION

stephanie stokes oliver

DOUBLEDAY
New York London Toronto Sydney Auckland

PUBLISHED BY DOUBLEDAY
a division of Random House, Inc.
1540 Broadway, New York, New York 10036

DOUBLEDAY and the portrayal of an anchor with a dolphin are trademarks of Doubleday, a division
of Random House, Inc.

Design by Mauna Eichner

Library of Congress Cataloging-in-Publication Data

Oliver, Stephanie Stokes.
    Seven soulful secrets for finding your purpose and minding your mission / Stephanie
Stokes Oliver.
        p. cm.
    1. Success—Psychological aspects. 2. Women—Psychology. I. Title: Seven soulful secrets.
II. Title.

BF637.S8 O45 2001
158.1—dc21
2001028325

ISBN 0-385-48767-3

First Edition

10   9   8   7   6   5   4   3   2   1

Love and gratitude from my heart and soul to

God
Who made all of us on purpose, for a purpose

My mother,
Josephine Stratman Stokes
Whose verve and purposeful life is our family's inspiration

My husband,
Reginald Oliver
A good man with whom I share a loving mission

C O N T E N T S

seven soulful secrets

INTRODUCTION

Quick—what is your life's purpose? If you think you know what it is, then you are more evolved than most people! If you don't know what it is, then this book will help you to name it and claim it. I can tell you this: If you are constantly trying to be your ultimate self, if you are always making an effort to "move on up a little higher," then you will find your purpose. And if you find your purpose, then the road you take to achieve it is your mission.

Most people call this "success." If "success" is a term that feels more comfortable to you than "purpose," feel free to use it. Whatever you call it, know that it is yours alone to claim. It's not your mama's, your man's, or your best friend's. It's a goal that is unique to you. You are one-of-a-kind, a divine original; your purpose is yours alone. And when you accomplish it, it will belong to you. It's your soul purpose and your sole purpose.

Purpose is when someone finally decides to dedicate herself to pursuing the craft of acting rather than following the well-intentioned advice of family to get a "secure job" at the post office. Because it's not *their* destiny, other people may not be able to understand your passion, let alone support it. You've got to believe in it for yourself. And then, believe me, when you do accomplish great things after following your own heart, all the naysayers will suddenly get amnesia: "Who me? I never said you couldn't do that!"

If we seek our purpose, everything else we desire will fall in line. We'll have success, because no one will be better able to do what we do. We'll have love, because we won't feel the need to depend on others to fulfill us. We'll have health and happiness, because we will always be willing to pursue our optimum fitness and well-being.

Following our ultimate purpose is the new way of defining success for the third millennium. "Being happy" is how futurist Faith Popcorn sees success in the years ahead. And isn't that the ultimate? Popcorn further describes how we'll be "cashing out, caring for kids. It's going to be the Women's Era. We won't separate leisure and work as much as we used to."

Success magazine once polled readers for their definition of "success." The answer: Good health.

With these trends in mind, I offer in the pages of this book a new guide for women to discover this exciting, more healthful reality. If you were the type of student who always got the "crib notes" instead of reading the entire book, you can check out the following cheat sheet of what is covered in the seven chapters of this book right here. But if you want the lasting pleasure that comes not from just scratching the surface, but from going deeper into your ultimate self, I invite you to read the rest of the book for the details, how-tos, and secrets of finding your purpose and minding your mission.

Here's how I spell out my seven soulful secrets of P-U-R-P-O-S-E:

Secret One: P Is for Purpose

A lot of people are afraid of pursuing their purpose. They think it means they have to be perfect, flawless. Or they feel it will require them to be squeaky clean, straight, square, corny. But perfect by whose measure? Maybe your purpose requires you to be totally eccentric in order to achieve it. For example, if you're a creative person, your style of dress or hair or way of pursuing your art may be so unique that you are regarded as being out of the mainstream. But the world needs that. We need a lot of tributaries—not just the main stream.

We can't always be what others want us to be. We can only be our-selves. When you are following your heart, when you are being true to your nature, you are pursuing your purpose. In this chapter, you will learn:

- How to find your purpose

- What the difference is between purpose and mission

- How to get other people to mind their own mission and leave yours alone

- How independent thinking is the key to being your best self

- How to love your work and your life

💘 Secret Two: U Is for Ultimacy 💘

Together we'll explore what makes a woman go from ordinary to ex-traordinary. What makes her soar to great heights? The achievement of being your ultimate self—what I'll call "ultimacy"—comes from getting to know yourself—and loving what you learn to know! It's self-motiva-tion that makes you "keep on pushin'" even when the going is tough. Ul-timacy means living your life in the state of being your ultimate, best self. It's reaching your utmost and celebrating the many facets of your-self that start with the letter U, such as being:

- Unique

- Unusual

- Unequaled

- Unbought and unbossed—as former Congresswoman Shirley Chisholm would say

💗 *Secret Three: R Is for Relaxation* 💗

First, check out the stress test. Find out just how stressed you are—or aren't! See if what you are experiencing is "good" stress or "bad" stress. There's a difference!

We'll talk about how to have an "adventure in bed," how to give yourself permission to relax and recharge by lounging around in bed once a week. You can have your "adventure" all day, or just get an extra hour of rest. We'll talk about what you desire, or need, to de-stress.

The latest status symbol is not a luxury car or a big house with a pool. It's something money can't buy: I am talking about sleep. "Forget about stock options, the ultimate perk for the truly successful is now eight hours' sleep," an article in *The Wall Street Journal* proclaimed. Well, I'm going to tell you how to get it even when you feel harried, stressed out, overworked, and underappreciated—in other words, normal. Whether you're a married mom trying to balance the two extremes of a high-pressure job and family responsibilities, or a single, child-free woman with a full plate of long working hours and elderly parents—or someone in between—you can find balance. We are all searching for the same thing: peace, quiet, alone time. Having been a young, single (party-heartying) professional and then a career-driven (too-pooped-to-party) mom, I know the pressures firsthand. And over the years I've fought hard to counteract them; so it's my pleasure to share with you what's worked for me. If there's one thing I'm good at, it's getting my R&R on! You can do it, too. In this chapter, you'll learn how.

💗 *Secret Four: P Is for Positivity* 💗

When we are positive, we believe, we hope, we expect, we achieve. Shaking off negativity and anger, we are more likely to be confident, to see humor in our situation, and to act assertively. These are qualities that make change happen.

And as change within or around us is happening, we can step back occasionally and celebrate.

In remembering the 1960s, I recall the seriousness of our struggle, how dedicated so many Americans were to the goal of equality for all. I remember the marches and the protests, many of which I participated in. But I also recall a whole lot of partying. During that time, we may have had to lead a protest during the day, but we often ended up "twisting the night away." Some of us counteracted and released our intense feelings of the struggle with an equally intense desire to party.

If pursuing our purpose is not a destination but a journey, then we need to take time from our constant striving to appreciate our accomplishments. You may not be able to give yourself an annual raise, but you can take yourself to lunch as an anniversary observance and celebrate yourself! You may not be able to give yourself a promotion, but you can buy yourself flowers for a job well done. And when you do get public recognition, how can you handle it with modesty, dignity, and humility? Turn to this chapter for tips on how to stay positive and claim the joy in your life.

In addition, you'll learn how to:

- Laugh to keep from crying

- Keep a joy journal

- Get "up" and stay positive when you feel "down"

- Avoid negaholics

- Join a secret society of happy people!

💮 *Secret Five: O Is for Optimum Health* 💮

I am convinced that one of the secrets of reaching our ultimacy is the commitment to seeking optimum health. It takes dedication to self-improvement, good health, and optimum fitness to reach our goals, whatever they may be. If we don't have our health, if we don't pursue the highest forms of nourishment for our minds, bodies, and souls, we fall short of reaching our highest potential and being our best self.

I've come up with a prescription for optimum health that outlines what I believe to be the most important aspects of health and well-being, and how to achieve them. I condensed what could have been volumes of health information and fitness research into a few points of reader-friendly advice. They come down to self-improvement in the areas of:

- Healthy habits
- Good nutrition
- Physical fitness
- Weight control
- Health advocacy

What's the number-one question of accomplished, achieving, busy women today? *How can I work fitness into my busy schedule?* I'll give you some answers, as well as tackle the second-most-asked question: *Now that I have the time, how do I stay motivated?*

The key to getting better, not just older, is self-improvement. And self-improvement is probably one of the biggest elements of optimum health. The pursuit of self-improvement doesn't mean there's something wrong that needs fixing. It means that a good thing can always get better, that we all need refresher courses in life. Think about this: Although Ford is a popular car, no one is still driving a Model T. Life involves change, and to adapt to it, we have to keep growing, to continue to learn, to expand our knowledge unceasingly, forever.

The "motor" that drives commitment to self-improvement is persistence and perseverance. Be sure to check out the tips on how to get your motor totally revved up.

Secret Six: S Is for Spirituality

Spirituality is the foundation for all the secrets that have come before in this book. It's the beginning and the end. It's the basis for all our success because it involves faith in the unrealized, the hoped for. One has to *believe* in one's success in order to achieve it. And in doing so, one has added a spiritual dimension to the task.

Do you know the difference between spirituality and religion? The difference between prayer and meditation? Those are some of the things you'll learn in this chapter on how to tap the power of spirituality to become your ultimate self.

In addition, I'll discuss one of the most important spiritual values of all—compassion—and how caring for others makes us better people.

Peace, quiet, serenity, and solitude are all important elements of success, as much as team building, office politics, and job sharing. We'll explore how to pursue those key elements when you have a busy, bustling life, bursting with children, a mate, a demanding boss, and relatives.

It all comes down to the way in which we end each day—the same way we start it—ever mindful of the divine spirit. Rest, meditation, and prayerfulness are all elements of our ultimate inner power. It is my prayer that this chapter will guide you toward the holistic health and high spirits you need to pursue the purpose you were born for.

❧ Secret Seven: E Is for Esteem ❧

Love your Creator, then love yourself. Love yourself, then you can love others. When I was the editor of *Heart & Soul* magazine, our researchers found that issues of self-esteem were at the top of the list of concerns of African American women. Like most people, we want to have the kind of self-love that protects us from being hurt by others. We all need to take care of ourselves, to nurture the loving spirit inside, and then let the reservoir overflow to others. We can't give from an empty spirit, but we have so much to share when our spirits are full and healthy and our "cup runneth over."

Not only do we aspire to have high self-esteem, we want to be held in high esteem by others: family, friends, lovers, the community. The morals, ethics, and standards we exhibit all play a part in the esteem we get back. Holding high standards in relationships can be the difference between loving, healthy relationships and difficult, even abusive, alliances. Most important, in choosing and insisting on wholesome relationships in all areas of our lives, we take control of our overall health. Worrying about a dangerous relationship is not healthy for us or for family members, who in turn worry about us. But difficult as it may be, taking charge of preventing abusive situations, or getting out of those we find ourselves in, will lower our blood pressure, relieve us of stress, and allow us to soar.

In addition, in this chapter, I've provided a quick quiz to help you assess your self-image. There are also seven soulful secrets of self-esteem provided by some folks held in high esteem themselves.

So there you have it:

Purpose

Ultimacy

Relaxation

Positivity

Optimum Health

Spirituality

Esteem

Finding your purpose is not a pie-in-the-sky concept. Like the love of the Creator, it's as close to you as your breath. It manifests who you were meant to be. It's being who you really are, not trying to be like anyone else or allowing anyone to define you. Reaching your full unique potential—whatever it is—is your purpose in life. And the path you take to do so is your mission. Enjoy the journey!

$\mathscr{P}$URPOSE

"Purpose" seems like such a lofty concept for most of us. It conjures up images of God talking to us in a grave tone, saying, "Here is what you were put on Earth to do." That's how I've heard some ministers describe how they got "the Calling," for example. But for the rest of us mere humans, "the Call" never comes. Or at least if it does, it isn't that dramatic.

For most of us, it takes a *long* time to find our purpose—if we ever find it at all. It's like looking for the proverbial needle in a haystack. In our moments of reflection, often brought on by despair, we wonder, *What am I here for? Why was I born?* It's easy to find out *when* you were born, but knowing *why* you were born can be one of life's challenges. Yet, like any great problem, it can be solved! And you'll be all the better for having done the soul-searching needed to find the answer.

If we look at the lives of great people, their purpose seems so clear. It could be said that Martin Luther King, Jr., was born to give this country—and the world—a vision of equality for all, and to work toward making it a reality. Yet he lived with doubt and insecurities brought on by the high cost of having that purpose. But his triumph was in never letting that adversity stop him from pursuing what was embedded in his soul.

Like many people in the civil rights movement, his purpose was backed by a mission to help people. King, my parents, maybe your grandparents, and others felt as the song goes: "If I can help some-body, . . . then my living shall not be in vain."

To help one person may appear to be a small goal, but any big thing starts with a small gesture, and that small gesture leads to another, and another. For example, you can start with yourself first by developing in-ner strength and outer character. Then, with that wholeness you can help someone else: a child perhaps, a mentee, an elder. With that suc-cess, you may be encouraged to teach school, lead a Scout troop, play piano for a church choir. As you mature, so will your mission.

Around the time I entered Franklin High School in Seattle, the stu-dent body president was a smart brother named Franklin Raines, whom I heard had a photographic memory and got straight As on his report cards all through high school. When he graduated magna cum laude from Harvard, he made news in our city by becoming a Rhodes Scholar. Continuing his ascent, he held groundbreaking jobs, including serving in the Clinton Administration as director of the White House Office of Management and Budget. In January 1999, he became the first African American to head a Fortune 500 company as chairman and CEO of FannieMae, the largest nonbank financial services company in the world.

Another dynamic young man was also a student leader of my high school the next year. Gary Locke went on to become the first Asian American governor of the State of Washington, and the first Asian Amer-ican to be a governor of a mainland U.S. state.

What Frank and Gary have in common is—not only my great high school!—but a track record of pursuing their own high purpose. As teenagers, they exhibited leadership. And as mature men, they are still leading. As their knowledge and experiences expanded, their areas of opportunity and influence did as well. Now they have gone from lead-ing high school assemblies to leading national forums. As they matured, so did their missions.

As you get older and wiser, your self-awareness will grow and maybe even amuse and surprise you. One day last year when I was out pro-moting my book *Daily Cornbread,* I had a revelatory experience that helped light the path of my own mission.

One of my good friends, Shelia Baynes, had generously organized a book party with some other friends, Joyce Harley, Linda Thomas, and Janice Carter, and the other members of their New Jersey book club, The Bibliophiles. The event fell on a crisp, fall Sunday afternoon. For me, the vibe from the moment I woke up made me feel that something special was in the air.

With my husband and daughter out of town, I started the day in prayer and solitude. I had decided not to go to church, so that I wouldn't be late for the event. Instead, I had "church" at home. I listened to Gospel music on the radio as I took a long meditative bath. During this bath, a childhood memory came to me that made me laugh.

Were you the "baby" of the family? I was. As the youngest, I had very little influence over my sister and brother. If we were playing "cowboys and Indians," André, my brother, was always the sheriff or the tribal chief. If we were playing "school," my sister, Vicki, was inevitably the teacher.

But somehow, whenever my siblings and I came home from Sunday services and took to occupying ourselves by playing "church" while our mother cooked brunch, I got to be the minister. No one else would touch that one. In our basement, we had an old pedestal-style coffee table. The top of it could lay flat or tilt at an angle, making a perfect pulpit just right for my four-year-old height. I would stand behind it and start slowly, calmly, and softly, as I'd seen the minister at Mount Zion do. By the end of my "sermon," I was animated and loud. Attempting to imitate the preacher's booming voice, I would holler, "And the Lord said, 'Let there be light!'" André and Vicki would be cracking up. To this day, whenever I tell Vicki about one of my Sunday speaking engagements, she asks, "Oh yeah? Well, did you preach?" And we both laugh.

When I arrived for the book party on this particular, more recent Sunday, I saw a friend of mine, Doris Boyer, who is a member of a church I formerly attended in New Jersey for many years. Catching me up on the happenings at the church, Doris told me about a new book club the church sisters were starting. "Yes," she said, "so now we have a book ministry!"

That idea took hold of me. A book ministry.

My grandfather, Norris J. Stokes, was a minister. During his tenure, the magnificent Second Baptist Church of Pratt, Kansas, was built and still stands. My father, Charles M. Stokes, had opted to be a Seattle attorney, but he held many leadership roles in our church and often joked that he must have missed his calling because, as he said, "Folks don't like to pay their attorney, but they always take care of their preacher."

When Doris said the words "book ministry," it all came together for me: my childhood antics, my heritage of ministry, and my passion to write books. I finally knew that I was fulfilling a mission. Pursuing a book ministry gave me a higher calling than just writing to satisfy my own creative urges. It fell perfectly within my purpose of striving to be a bright light, beaming information and inspiration for human improvement.

💚 *Finding Your Purpose* 💚

First, to know how to find it, you have to know what "it" is. As a wordsmith, I always enjoy looking up words. Even if it's a word we use often in common language, I find that there are sometimes hidden meanings we either don't consider or take for granted. In looking up "purpose" in my Franklin Bookman electronic dictionary, I find it says simply:

1. something aimed at

2. resolution

3. what one proposes to accomplish or do

What are you aiming for? What do you propose to accomplish or do in this life? If you are blessed with longevity, perhaps there will be several things you'd like to accomplish. You may have career goals that can serve a higher need within your spirit. For example, if you are a person who makes lots of money as a stockbroker, you may have a purpose of using that money for the greater good of humanity through philanthropy and charity. Then again, if you want to be a successful comedian, it might be your purpose to bring more laughter into this often somber world.

So, just how do you find your purpose?

Take a stab in the dark. Step out on faith. Search your soul. Whether you use a journal, notebook, PC, or PDA to record your innermost thoughts, take it out and ask yourself these questions:

What are the things that give my soul satisfaction? What would you pursue that your best friend, family member or lover, wouldn't? If there's an area of your life in which you feel fulfilled or particularly passionate about, it's probably a clue to your unique purpose.

Our family friend, Dorothy Pitman Hughes, lives and breathes the work she does in Harlem. As a community activist and owner of the Harlem Copy Center, located smack in the middle of world-famous 125th Street and just a few blocks east of the Apollo Theater, she is committed to seeing that her beloved community gets its fair share of government funds, gentrification, and business support. Dorothy is passionate about the empowerment of Harlem. She exudes her purpose.

What is my nature? Are you always dancing or singing? Do you like to draw or paint? Maybe you don't feel you have a unique talent, but do you think you have a skill at fostering the talents of others?

Vivian Ayers, the mother of talented dancer/actor/choreographer Debbie Allen, recognized the talent of her daughter at a young age. "When I was five my mother saw that I could be a great dancer," Debbie said to me in an interview I conducted for *Essence*. "So she helped make it happen for me. If she had let it slide, I might be in a real different place right now."

Fortunately for all of us, Ms. Ayers not only didn't let it slide when it came to Debbie, but also encouraged Debbie's sister, Phylicia Rashad, who also had a passion for the arts. Phylicia found her fame as the television wife of Bill Cosby. Debbie, who starred in the television show *Fame,* became a choreographer of the Academy Awards program and the producer for the movie *Amistad.*

The description Debbie gave of her mother nurturing her talent had a personal impact on me. My own daughter was a preschooler around the time of my interview with Debbie, and my husband and I had recently come to the realization that our Anique also was a gifted dancer.

Following Ms. Ayers' example, I decided to make a difference in my child's life. I enrolled Anique in dance classes.

Lessons were offered at our local public school system's Saturday arts program, so they were affordable and allowed us to see if our instincts were right. When the dance teacher called us to make sure Anique would be in the year-end recital so that she could lead the other children, we knew we were on target. As she progressed, we wanted to see how she would fare if she was able to study under a more rigorous dance curriculum. Taking advantage of our proximity to New York City, we took her to audition for the children's division of Alvin Ailey American Dance Theater. When Alvin Ailey himself commented on her talent in the last children's recital before his passing, we felt Anique had been given his blessing. With the help of supportive family and friends who drove her several days a week after school from New Jersey into New York, along with some creative budgeting on our part, Anique continued with Ailey for another ten years. And now, she attends Debbie and Phylicia's alma mater (which is also my own), Howard University.

Yolanda Adams' unique musical talent as a Gospel singer won her a Grammy Award. Adams is not embarrassed to talk about her purpose. In a 2001 interview with me for NiaOnline, she talked unblinkingly about it.

"My purpose is to bring as much joy to the hearts of people as possible," she said. "If today is not a good day, tomorrow holds more promise. My goal is to let people know there is good in all of us. And that good comes out when you know God. When you think R&B, you think it's all about the love between a man and woman. This music is about the love of God and of self. My purpose is to get the music out to the people who need it."

If you have it in your nature to do something, it might just be your purpose. If you have a gift, it is also a gift to the world.

What is my passion? If there is a thing that you do whenever you get a chance, that you can't wait to do day after day, that you think about and obsess about, it may be your passion.

Of course, passion is usually a word used to describe our strong feelings of affection for someone we desire. But you can also have a passion for fashion or for shopping. And although it may not seem on the surface that either one could translate into a high purpose, consider the story of Nancy Lublin.

Born into privilege in New York City, Lublin turned her love of fashion into a crusade to help low-income women look good and feel confident in job interviews. "How can you pull yourself up by your bootstraps if you don't have boots?" asks Nancy Lublin, the twenty-nine-year-old founder and executive director of Dress for Success, her nonprofit organization that provides interview suits to low-income women seeking employment. (She is on the Web at *www.dressforsuccess.org.*)

Dress for Success was founded in 1996 when Lublin, a third-year law student at New York University, inherited $5,000 from her great-grandfather, "Poppy Max." An immigrant from Eastern Europe, Poppy Max spent his first two weeks in the United States sleeping under the Brooklyn Bridge. Then he built a business in the garment industry by peddling clothes out of a cart during the Depression. To help those in need, he developed a layaway payment system. Inspired by his compassion, Ms. Lublin founded Dress for Success.

Conversely, there are those of us who know where our passions lie, but are afraid to pursue them. "Many of us avoid our passion," says Joann Tolbert-Yancy, an author and public speaker who lives near Dallas, Texas. "I wanted to talk for a living, but I didn't think I was good enough."

Joann, a tall and beautiful woman with deep-brown, flawless skin, was saying this before a group of about one hundred women gathered at a Barnes & Noble in Richmond, California, in March 2000. She had sounded full of self-confidence beginning her talk and had refused to use the mike because of her strong voice. As I heard her speak of overcoming her fears, it seemed hard to believe that she had ever had any. "Avoid negative self-talk," she advised the crowd.

Gloria Brown of San Lorenzo, California, also a motivational speaker, was the spirited moderator of the event. Her advice: "Follow your purpose by pursuing your passion, and you will find prosperity and peace."

Where do my interests lie? If you love animals, for example, you may be more compelled than others to advocate for animal rights. Or perhaps to work in a zoo. I know a young woman who worked in the Woodland Park Zoo in Seattle. Her interest and love of animals led her to want to protect and care for them.

Jacquelyn Hughes Mooney of New Orleans, Louisiana, turned her interest in quiltmaking into a high purpose. As artist-in-residence of the African American Women on Tour conference, she travels around the country helping women to express themselves by contributing an appliqué to a "dream quilt." In each city, attendees can bring a three-by-three-inch patch, which are then sewn together to make a finished quilt. Designed by Jackie, the quilts are colorful works of art that tell stories of triumph and inspiration. Beads, shells, photo-imaging, embroidery, fringe, buttons, bells, lace, and African fabrics are just some of the materials that add to the creativity. In each city, the quilts and the proceeds from monetary contributions are donated to nonprofit halfway houses and shelters.

In her work, Jackie says she uses only black thread, to signify "the common thread that holds us together." In addition, her use of purple "represents spirituality and royalty. Purple is the highest vibration in the color spectrum." It symbolizes, Jackie explains, "our desire to reach and search the highest forms of ourselves."

What experiences have shaped my life? Sometimes devastating events in our lives can become the catalyst for our finding our purpose. Someone who has seen racial oppression firsthand might be compelled to speak out against it at every turn. Another person who has witnessed or been a victim of domestic violence can be relentless in shaping public opinion and gaining needed support for victims.

Growing up in segregated Birmingham, Alabama, had a profound effect on political activist Angela Davis. In 1970 she went into hiding after a gun legally registered to her was used in an attempted courtroom escape in which a judge, young activist Jonathan Jackson, and two others were killed. Apprehended two months later, she spent months in prison before she was acquitted. Now a college professor in California, Davis is also a passionate spokesperson for prison reform.

Cornel West, the esteemed author and professor of Afro American Studies at Harvard University, is very clear about his purpose. Watching him in an interview on C-SPAN's *Booknotes* program, I counted that he expressed his purpose three times within the hour. First he said, "I'm a brother trying to make the world better than he found it by the time he exits the planet." Then, "I'm fighting for the voices of everyone to be heard—vis-à-vis the voices of the few." Last, in response to the question "Do you see yourself as a great philosopher?" West answered humbly, "I'm just a brother from the block trying to love somebody and make some sense before I die."

To some, West's references to death could appear to sound morbid, but what I picked up is that these thoughts comprise his life's mission. He is expressing what he is trying to accomplish during his lifetime: making a difference, helping the disenfranchised to have a voice in the world, being a loving person. In addition, he self-deprecatingly expressed his desire to "make some sense," or have his profound philosophies appeal to others, to have people understand him and relate to what he is saying enough to effect change.

Notice that your purpose doesn't always have to translate into your *job*. For many reasons, most of us aren't fortunate enough to work at jobs we love or have a passion for. If we are lucky, we might work at a job that expresses what our souls would have us do. Mothers who can afford to stay home with their young children may feel it is their purpose to be available and to shape their children's lives in this way. If someone is a hairstylist, she may feel that it is her purpose to make others feel beautiful.

Have you ever felt like an outsider? If you have, it could mean that you are an independent thinker, which means you have a unique purpose. Author Jamaica Kincaid and TV host Oprah Winfrey have said they each grew up without encouragement to be the booklovers we know them to be today. Jamaica Kincaid wrote in her book *A Small Place* that when she was a child she took refuge under her raised house in Antigua to be able to read books in peace.

The woman who is credited with getting millions of nonreading television viewers to buy books was made to feel like an outsider in her own family because of her love of books as a child. "Not only was my mother not a reader," Oprah Winfrey told *Life* magazine in 1997, "but I remember being in the back hallway when I was about nine—I'm going to try to say this without crying—and my mother threw the door open and grabbed a book out of my hand and said, 'You're nothing but a something-something bookworm. Get your butt outside! You think you're better than the other kids.' I was treated as though something was wrong with me because I wanted to read all the time." Oprah's mother, Vernita, admitted on an A&E television biography that she didn't want her daughter to be different from other kids in the neighborhood. She thought she should spend more time outdoors.

In a story similar to Oprah's, a fifth-grade teacher almost succeeded in making another child feel as though something was wrong with her for her independent love of reading. The author of *The Inscription,* Pam Binder, is an office manager in Issaquah, Washington, who pursues her lifelong obsession with writing at lunchtime, after work, at night, anytime, and everywhere. A story in the *Seattle Times* recounts that her teacher told her mother, "Pam's reading too much. She's reading during recess." Her mother retorted that she didn't consider her daughter's love of reading grounds for complaint.

It is helpful to have a supporter as Pam did, because it can be sad and hurtful to be considered an outsider. But turn it around to look at it this way: If you think "outside the box," it just means that you are an independent thinker, something that this country does value. The outsiders of yesterday become the movers and shakers of tomorrow. If your "outsider" pursuit is something positive, you can turn it into a positive force. To make a difference, you've got to *be* different.

💚 The Difference Between 💚 Purpose and Mission

Purpose is the manifestation of your highest self. It means being in touch with your personal power and a vision of greater good.

Your *mission* is the way you carry out your purpose. It's the road map to your destination. It's how you accomplish your goal.

Growing up in the turbulent 1960s, I was an admirer of Stokely Carmichael, who later changed his name to Kwame Ture. A self-described revolutionary, Ture aroused the passions of many in this country by popularizing the term "Black Power!" I don't know what Ture, who died in the late 1990s, would have said his purpose was, but it seems to me that he was meant to shed light on the oppressive treatment of African Americans and to empower us to do something about it. His mission in doing this was to organize black people in America and in Africa, where he eventually made his home, into what he called a Pan-African movement. Ture wrote a book called *Black Power*. He talked about the concept of collective and self-empowerment wherever he went in the world; he was relentless. So much so that some friends and loved ones implored him to slow down to concentrate on his health when he was diagnosed with prostate cancer. But he wouldn't be slowed—this man's life work was his life's purpose. And he was on a mission to spread his message until the day he died.

We Came to Serve

One hint to finding your purpose is to think of it in terms of serving others. We are all here for the purpose of loving and serving each other. So, our individual purpose is an offshoot of our collective purpose. Serving others makes your own contribution go beyond just serving yourself. It makes a contribution to the *world*—not just to you. In turn, your reward will be greater and bigger than you can imagine. You will not only grow and evolve within your purpose yourself, you will benefit others and they will grow and evolve as well, and those people will touch others who will benefit—all making the world a better place. As the Spiritual goes, "If I can help somebody . . . then my living shall not be in vain."

Don't worry if your mission changes as time goes by. If your mission is the road to your purpose, then think of any changes as just going in another direction. Just like two people may give you two different directions for getting to the same place, there may be several paths to the same destination. None are necessarily better than another—just different, maybe more difficult, perhaps more fun. Change is good. It broadens our horizons, it keeps us alert and interested. It makes life exciting. It helps if we can keep mustering enthusiasm for our purpose. Accomplishing one mission, then tackling another, is one way to do it.

Dreaming is another. Your daydreams and your imaginings are only life's longing for what can be. Nothing new is created without first having been an idea in someone's head. The mind's ability to envision something that does not exist is nothing short of awesome.

Allow yourself to revel in your dreams. The visions in your inner eye allow you to see your potential. They aren't just unattainable ideals; they're what can be. They are what your heart longs for and what your mind plans to do.

When I travel on airplanes, my head is "in the clouds." For some reason, being up so high from my earthly concerns allows my thoughts to soar. I always sit by the window, and looking out on the great expanse makes my mind feel free to dream big. My thoughts are clearer, more concise, especially on long cross-country flights. While flying, I have made many solid decisions and thought up lots of creative ideas that have moved my life forward.

Back down to Earth, I find it helpful to try to replicate my feeling of flying by driving to the Eagle Rock Reservation's mountaintop observation area near my town in New Jersey. From there I can see the New York City skyline and can think about the reasons I came to pursue my purpose in the Big Apple. At my mother's home in Seattle, I can look out at her hilltop view of Lake Washington and Mount Rainier and allow myself to swallow doubt and feel as though there is no mountain I can't climb. For me, going home is like returning to the womb—where I had nine months to form my thoughts.

For a girlfriend of mine who lives in a northern urban center, the place to dream is at her grandmother's farm in the South. For my husband, it's in his home office, where after a day's work he turns off all the lights and meditates for twenty minutes. Do you have a special place where your mind can be at ease, where you can dream up all kinds of ways to pursue your purpose and map out your mission? It can be as special as an ancestral home or as accessible as the nearest easy chair. Wherever it is, name it, claim it, and call it your own.

TRY THIS EXERCISE:

- Get quiet. Lie down or sit uninterrupted in your favorite cozy chair.

- Let your mind drift. What are your biggest, highest imaginings? Try to envision yourself within that scenario.

- Think of yourself doing something that makes you happy and also serves others. Write down your vision of yourself doing your greatest good.

- Then at the bottom of the page, write "BELIEVE" in cap letters. Then believe that you can do it.

The singer R. Kelly believes he can fly. By articulating his vision of himself through his music and the song "I Believe I Can Fly," this singer inspires others to believe their spirits can soar, too. What do *you* believe you can do?

Taking time to reflect is just as important as all the time it takes to be busy. Thinking that we have to "get up and go" is well and good—we do have to take action and make things happen. But it is also necessary to get quiet in order to be at peace with what action we have to take. Often, all the running around we do is more like an idle motor. We're moving, but going nowhere. Like the engine of a car, we experience times when we just need to turn off the idle motor and sit still. When we're not getting anywhere fast anyway, it's best to turn off the noise, save the energy, park yourself in a good spot, and chill. In these moments of relaxation, a solution to all you have been busying yourself about just may come to you. You may decide to take a different path, try a new tactic, learn a helpful skill, develop another talent, seek greater knowledge. Then again, you may make the decision to do nothing. We say this often: Let go and let God. That's alright, too.

❦ *Follow Your Intuition* ❦

When you get quiet and allow yourself to dream and visualize, you are developing insight. Break down that word: "in" and "sight." You are developing inner sight; seeing deeply into your interior world of wants, desires, potential, and growth. When you act on your insight, you are following your intuition.

One thing about insight and intuition is that no one can pursue them for you. You can't cheat on the test. You can borrow someone else's notes, but the ultimate insight of how to move your life forward has to be your very own. You can fool some folks, but you can't fool yourself. You know if you are being real. "To thine own self be true," as Shakespeare said, still holds true. "Keeping it real" is the hip-hop way of saying the same thing. No matter how you say it, only you can determine if you are being authentic.

Acting on your inner voice—even when it seems contrary to what other people are doing—is always okay. Especially when the force behind it is positive. Your intuition tells you what is right for *you*. When you say, "*Something told me* to go this way instead of that way," you are saying that your intuition is doing its thing. When you think, *I had a feeling that was the right answer,* you are articulating your inner soulful response. When you declare, "*I knew* I should have zigged instead of zagged!" you are expressing gut feeling. Don't look for others to validate your intuition, your inner response, your gut feeling. Gather your courage, and strength, and step out on faith.

❦ *Risky Business* ❦

To take a risk means that we are willing to chance loss or gain. It's just as likely that following our intuition could lead to a gain as a loss, and much of the time we have nothing to lose. If you haven't taken any steps toward realizing your goal, you don't have anything to risk losing.

What you want to take are *calculated* risks. You want to calculate how much you could lose, and if it's worth it; to add up the consequences and then do what needs to be done.

For example, starting a business should always be a calculated risk. One shouldn't up and quit their job until they are in the position to actually succeed in making a business work. That means seriously studying the business you want to start, learning about self-employment taxes, and how to set up an effective accounting system. It might be wise to do the business on the side while you are holding down a job that pays the bills until your own business makes enough to sustain you. Then when you're finally ready to make a move from the comfortable employment of working for someone else to the uncertainty of working for yourself, the risk will seem less daunting. That's what calculated risk taking is all about.

Beyond believing enough in your intuition to act on your dreams, you need to back up your beliefs with concrete facts, figures, knowledge, study, research. Then, when you begin to make your dream a reality, it will be built on a firm foundation.

I know someone who was once a well-respected and accomplished book editor. One day, to the astonishment of many who knew her, Marie Brown left her job to start a magazine. When word got out that she would be quitting, people wondered why she would want to leave one of the most prestigious publishing companies in New York City when there weren't many African American book editors of her stature. Toni Morrison had already left a similar publishing position, and even though Morrison became an award-winning writer, she still left a void on the publishing side. Now this. Who would be left to fight for the publication of black books?

To further rock Brown's faith, the magazine she left to start soon folded. "I considered other book-publishing positions," Brown says, "but I eventually saw this interim period between jobs as one that would give me the opportunity to pursue my dream of working in a bookstore, which would give me the experience to open my own store. However, when I saw what it would take to do it right—mainly capital, and lots of it—I postponed that dream."

This smart and talented woman followed her insight and decided to work in a bookstore. In spite of the lack of validation for her choice ("Yes," Brown says, "people did doubt my wisdom in working in the store"), she enjoyed her two years there, first as a clerk, then assistant buyer, and assistant manager. Then, when she was ready to make her next move, she says there was still pressure to go back to her job as a book editor to "represent." But she had begun to notice that a trend was occurring: More and more publishers were requiring that authors be represented by agents. She decided to open a literary agency.

"It was a very difficult decision to get out there and make an attempt to start a business without the material support," Brown says about her shortage of venture capital, "not to mention the lack of spiritual and emotional support from most of the members of my family and some close friends." But now, looking back over more than a decade in business, Brown can feel proud of her accomplishments in advocating for the publication of African American literature. As one of the premier literary agents in the country, Marie Brown is living her dream, serving others, and making a difference. "All in all, this has been a highly rewarding experience."

Growing When You're Grown

Learning to take risks, understanding your purpose, and minding your mission are all things that happen as a result of mental and spiritual growth. As adults, we may have stopped growing physically, but we must continue to grow in mind and spirit. Living should mean learning.

You can have a Ph.D. by the time you are thirty years old. Does that mean you have learned all there is to know? Not hardly. Then again, some people who may not have had the opportunity to go on to higher education have acquired "street smarts." No matter what our scholastic achievements, we always have the capacity for growth.

When we continue to seek knowledge, we become wiser. The more knowledge we acquire, the more likely we will feel equipped to make life-changing decisions.

Here are some ways in which we can seek growth:

- *Study.* We don't have to stay in school to learn. If you want to acquire a new skill, or gain more knowledge on a subject, there are all kinds of adult classes, called "continuing education," to pursue. Ask at your local library or university for programs in your area. For spiritual growth, Sunday school may sound like child's play, but Bible study is just another name for the same thing. I know people who have read the Bible many times, yet they still find enlightenment in going to classes in which they study Scripture. There's a course, a class, a seminar, or workshop for just about any area in which you would like to grow. I should know—I've taken quite a few myself. Through the Learning Annex in New York City, I've studied calligraphy, sought spirituality, and learned how to promote my books.

- *Learn a new skill.* Women and men of all ages are learning how to use the Internet. That knowledge can help a person learn other talents and skills with the information that can be found on the Web. You're never too old to learn something new: how to play an instrument, speak a foreign language, or take up a sport.

- *Meet new people.* We grow in knowledge of each other by making new friends. People of other cultures and all ages help us to understand the world better, and give us the sense that we are not the center of the universe. Travel expands our outlook. And being open to getting to know someone whom you've recently met, makes you open to learning—not only about that person but about yourself. For example, you might be introduced to a new cuisine, and maybe that diet is more healthful than the one you are used to. So you benefit from learning a few recipes from a person who comes from another culture. You may expand your mind by forging a friendship with a person who is younger or older than you. Or you could learn some spiritual lessons as you listen to tales of different religions. Even if you have no desire to convert to another religion, there is always something beautiful and insightful to learn when you share conversation with someone whose spiritual beliefs differ from yours.

- *Read more.* For years, I kept hearing the word *"Ayurveda"* tossed around in the media, but didn't know what it meant. And then one night, I had a dream that I was learning all about *Ayurveda* and benefiting from it. Now I am gathering all the information that I can about this ancient Indian healing tradition that aims to prevent illness and to balance the mind, body, and spirit. As I do for just about everything I want to learn more about, I seek pertinent information wherever I can find it. Books, magazines, the Internet, newspapers, all have the capacity to set us on the path to growth.

• *Seek solitude.* You can learn so much about yourself when you take time to be alone. When your mind is not influenced by the routine sounds of your life, such as the radio, the passing traffic, the talk show, the telephone, the TV, you just may find that great thoughts have a chance to surface and your best work can emerge. *Roots* author Alex Haley sought solitude on Navy freighters. Poet Maya Angelou checks into a hotel in the town in which she lives to find inspiration and to write. Author Alice Walker goes to her house in the country. The late Duke Ellington, attired in a smoking jacket, would take to his bed to become inspired. Legend has it that jazz great John Coltrane went into his attic with his saxophone and just sat there looking at it. Many hours later, he emerged with his masterpiece, "A Love Supreme." Do you know where you need to go to grow?

• *Learn from your mistakes.* No one wants to make mistakes, but our frailties stretch us on out there. Look at failure not as something to be ashamed of, but as a stepping-stone to your next success. All great people have had missteps and mistakes. Try to see the lesson in the bad things that happen, then take your time to restrategize and turn your setback into a comeback.

   Didn't Vanessa Williams do a phenomenal job of showing the world how tenacity, persistence, and self-confidence can overcome even a humiliating mistake? After she was crowned Miss America— the first African American to win that title—nude photos surfaced that had been taken of her a few years before, and Vanessa was forced to give up her title of Miss America. At the same time that she was being ridiculed in the media, she was focusing her energy on developing her talents—the very skills that helped her become the first black Miss America. In Vanessa's case, she learned from her mistake, and so did a lot of other people. Women learned not to trust fast-talking photographers. Vanessa triumphed over her error, and proved that one can emerge bigger and better than before. She was on a mission that was more profound than her mistake.

- *Be involved in the lives of children.* Few things in life contribute to your capacity to grow in patience, tolerance, maturity, and love than childrearing. Not many of us consider the benefits of parenting when we conceive, but giving birth has a major effect on how we see the world. It is my belief that after women bring life into the world, they become more likely to want peace on Earth for the preservation of humanity. Children make us abandon our own juvenile ways in order to acquire the maturity it takes to be a good example for them. They encourage us to be the best people we can be. Rearing children encourages us to evaluate our morals, to take better care of ourselves, to plan for a more secure future. As our children's bodies grow, we grow in the wisdom it takes to guide them to a whole and healthy life. Of course, we can learn from them, as well. And we don't have to give birth to benefit. Whether we are stepparents, aunties, babysitters, scout leaders, neighbors, or teachers, the children in our lives have much to teach us about loving and laughing.

Think of growth in terms of your favorite flower. Flowers grow and blossom. Plant the seeds for your purpose and your mission. Keep nourishing these seeds, and they will grow and blossom, making you and the world around you a more beautiful place. As the saying goes, "the flower that blooms in adversity is a beautiful thing."

When Other People Are Not Living in Their Purpose

To grow in spirit and in health, we need to surround ourselves with people who are either already pursuing their purpose, or who are striving to find it. You may not know what form a person's purpose takes or what path they have chosen for their mission, but you can tell if someone is living positively. You can tell if someone is seeking higher ground—or trying to take others down. Unfortunately, there are many people who live their lives in the latter zone. Of course, you're not one of them or you wouldn't be reading this book. But because those negative people can have a big influence on the rest of us, it's worth taking a look at how they operate. Don't allow someone to misguide your mission.

Many negative people honestly feel that they have good intentions by holding you back. They claim they are keeping you from getting hurt, or taking a risk, or getting in trouble. In other words, they are telling you not to do anything they wouldn't do. In reality, they may be stopping you from doing what you think is right, or from following your own spirit. No matter how accomplished one becomes, we always remember the people who didn't believe in us, who tried to turn us around, who kept us back.

One famous example is told by Malcolm X in his autobiography. In 1940 as an eighth-grader in Boston, Malcolm expressed to his teacher an interest in becoming a lawyer.

"Mr. Ostrowski looked surprised," Malcolm, who was one of the school's top students, recalled in the book. "He kind of half-smiled and said, 'Malcolm, one of life's first needs is for us to be realistic. Don't misunderstand me, now. We all here like you, you know that. But you've got to be realistic about being a nigger. A lawyer—that's no realistic goal for a nigger. You need to think about something you *can* be. You're good with your hands—making things. Everybody admires your carpentry shop work. Why don't you plan on carpentry? People like you as a person— you'd get all kinds of work.' "

Now, there's nothing wrong with being a carpenter—Jesus was a carpenter, and He definitely got "all kinds of work" that He put to a higher purpose. But Malcolm wanted to be a lawyer, which we all now know would have been a perfect profession for him. Like his contemporaries Thurgood Marshall and Patricia Roberts Harris, who did become distinguished lawyers, he proved to have the oratorical and debating skills, as well as the passion and fire, that make a great attorney. Ironically, although Malcolm did not realize that particular ambition, his life's work involved what lawyers do—advocating on behalf of his people. No one can hold you back from achieving the purpose you were placed on earth to fulfill.

Have you ever had a Mr. Ostrowski in your life? Someone you felt was fond of you and meant you well, but lacked faith in you? When that happens, it hurts. And it's confusing. What at first may sound like concern but is really a putdown. It must have been painful for Malcolm, since as an adult he still recalled the slight that his grade-school teacher had made many years earlier. Unfortunately, everyone doesn't have the same vision for you that you have for you. In spite of what others think or say, you have to push on and hold on to *your* dreams.

There are many reasons why others can't always see your purpose and support it. In Malcolm's teacher's case, it was racism that blinded him. In someone else's case, it might be jealousy, envy, lack of faith, or just plain shortsightedness.

It may be insecurity that drives others to withhold their support and encouragement. I read of a young woman whose mother wouldn't help her get the tutoring she needed after school. After much anxiety over the situation, it was revealed that because the mother hadn't had the opportunity to finish high school, she harbored the feeling that her daughter might one day think she was smarter or better than her mother. The moral of that tale is that many times the reasons people don't support you say more about *them* than about you.

But it's often hard to ignore the lack of support. It makes us second-guess our feelings. We begin to believe that they are right and we are wrong. Particularly if your dream is to do something extraordinary, others are likely to only see it as "out of the ordinary," something to be rejected, something that may be done, but not by you. If our pursuit doesn't fit the neat and expected role others have determined is right for us, the things that "everybody else is doing," then it's suspect. Then *we* are suspect.

And if you admire and also depend on the person advising you, it hurts all the more. Many a marriage has dissolved because one spouse didn't support the growth of the other. Wives who want to go back to school but are held back by their husbands. Men who dream of pursuing their art or starting businesses but are pressured by women to "get a real job." It happens every day. There are a whole lot of folks who feel unfulfilled. When those closest to them are on a purposeful path, they feel left behind or intimidated. Instead of encouraging you to grow, they remain more comfortable trying to hold you back. Their intimidation factor makes them feel superior, but supremacy never wins. It's exploitative, it's manipulative, and controlling. Their greatest fear is that you may *succeed*. Then you will really be out of their control. If one were to operate from a higher plane, one would seek his or her own supreme consciousness. You can tell who the people are who pursue their purpose, because they want everyone else around them to do the same. They are so excited about the prospects for their own future, they want to motivate you to achieve your personal goals as well.

When You Are One of "Those People"

But of course, *you* are not one of those people, now are you? If we want others to believe in us, we need to believe in others. To paraphrase your mama, if you can't say something to encourage someone else, don't say anything at all. Even if you think an idea is outrageous, most of the time it's unnecessary to even comment on it. How many people take action on half the things they talk about? If you know in your heart someone's idea is really harmless, it's best to keep your negative comments to yourself. I don't mean to imply that you should be phony and say you love some cockamamie idea when you don't, but you don't have to slam someone's dreams for no reason either. You know the saying—what goes around, comes around . . .

I had this challenge a few years ago when my young daughter was asked what she wanted to be when she grew up. Like Malcolm told his teacher, I had hoped she'd say "an attorney," or a dancer, since she had spent so many years (and a lot of my money) in dance classes. But she surprised her father and me by saying she wanted to own a nightclub. We didn't take it very well.

"You don't need a college degree to own a nightclub," my husband said. "You could be a lawyer and still own a club."

I tried to be more diplomatic. "Maybe you could say you want to be an entrepreneur in the entertainment industry."

She took that advice and wrote that on her college application on the line where she was asked what her career goal was. But I had to grapple with my feelings that this nightclub ownership idea did not match the high aspirations we had in mind for her. That it didn't reflect well on us somehow, as if we would be perceived as having encouraged her to have low expectations. Eventually, after giving it more thought, I considered what role models she might have for nightclub ownership and I remembered the tales of Bricktop, the African American in Paris whose nightspots were the talk of the town, and Regine, who had a fabulous eponymous club on New York City's Park Avenue in the 1970s. Even Ian Schrager, one of the founders of the infamous Studio 54, now owns respectable and elegant hotels in New York, Miami, and Los Angeles. Heaven knows whether our daughter will end up owning the Cotton Club of the new millennium. If so, we'll be the first ones there partying with her! And knowing Anique, she'll say, "I told you so!"

Although age and experience give us a certain wisdom, goals and aspirations of our children come from more "advanced" thinking. As Kahlil Gibran says in *The Prophet,* we need to acknowledge that children "dwell in the house of tomorrow, which you cannot visit, not even in your dreams." And that we need to strive to be more like our children than have them be like us. Life moves forward. Every second, every minute, every day, moves ahead. Bill Gates's parents weren't too happy to hear him say he wanted to drop out of college to work with computers. But his vision was that of the next generation.

Remember when someone didn't support your dream? You will be recalled in the same way if you slam-dunk another person's goal. When you disapprove, turn it into a lesson for yourself. Do you have any feelings of jealousy or envy? Are insecurities or feelings of abandonment keeping you from wholly embracing your loved one's purpose? For example, if your young-adult child wants to move away to another part of the country to take a job or go to school, do you criticize the plan when your real feelings are that you don't want to be separated from your child? And if you are honest in saying you don't want to be alone, how does that further your child's goals and plans? It doesn't.

Don't let *your* needs stifle the positive pursuits of others. Don't make loved ones feel guilty for having high ambitions to accomplish something that the world may need. Put those greater needs—the gifts that person you love has to bring the world—ahead of your fears of feeling less loved. That's what strength is about. You might remember that the columns of a building need to stand apart to hold up the ceiling. Less togetherness might make you more self-reliant, as well as helping the other person pursue his or her dream. And when you are alone, you may be more in tune with the desires and needs of your own heart and soul.

💟 Collective Purpose 💟

If we can accept the unique contributions each of us brings to the world and support one another's purpose, then we will be brought closer together. In interactions across racial lines, we would "come together," to use a Beatles phrase. We call it "unity" (and as fate would have it, the word unity is contained within the word comm*unity*). Coming together for a common purpose is what the African American holiday season of Kwanzaa is all about. One of the seven principles that defines the core values and consciousness of the cultural celebration is *Nia*—Swahili for "purpose."

Defined by Maulana Karenga, the founder of Kwanzaa, *Nia* represents the value of making "a commitment to the collective vocation of the building and developing of our community in order to restore our people to their traditional greatness." Following the belief that as African descendants, we are the heirs to the mothers and fathers of humanity and civilization, Karenga implores us in his book *Kwanzaa: A Celebration of Family, Community and Culture* to see "our purpose in light of our historical and cultural identity." And to preserve the legacy by guarding it, honoring it, promoting it, and expanding it. In so doing, we can leave an enriched legacy for future generations.

Nia, a kind of community purpose, can give us guidelines for our personal purpose as well. We get so much more out of giving to others and trying to make the world a better place than we do from merely pursuing private goals—say, to make money or have material things. Some historical figures who can serve as role models for the *Nia* spirit include Harriet Tubman, who not only escaped her bondage as a slave herself, but made it her mission to return to the South repeatedly to help others to freedom, risking her own life with each trip. Mary McLeod Bethune sought an education, not for her own personal gain, but to establish a college that would educate others. Ida B. Wells didn't start a newspaper just to make money to buy a big house; she did so to have a voice against lynching. True greatness rarely occurs in isolation. Those that become great make contributions to the world. Like Cornel West suggested, they make contributions that leave the world a better place than they found it. If our purpose is always framed within the context of the needs, hopes, and aspirations of our larger family, community, society, and the world, then we are truly guided by the spirit of *Nia*.

Recently, the spirit of *Nia* guided a team of like-minded souls (of which I am a part) to name a new Web site. Our mission was to find a name that would express the high aspirations of African American women. Our site would inform and inspire, providing everything from parenting tips to breaking news. We wanted our site to be positive, personal, and passionate, with practical information to help the user become more prosperous *and* peaceful. Searching the Web, we investigated domain names to see which ones were available. We tried Aspire.com, Inspire.com, Strive.com, Soar.com, Wings.com, Affirm.com, and more. All were taken. Then we tried more Afrocentric names: Sheba.com, AfricanQueen.com, Amandla.com, and Sahara.com (there's Amazon, so we'd be Sahara—get it?). Again, no luck. Finally, we tried Nia.com. That was the Web site of the National Insular Association, the NIA. Inspired by NetNoir, we tried NiaNet. The NIA had that, too. We kept trying to come up with something that would include the word *Nia* because we liked the concept of providing a site for women of purpose. We tried again with NiaOnline—bingo!

Of course, before people started naming Web sites, people were naming babies. As the cultural celebration of Kwanzaa has become more widespread, Nia has become a more popular African American name. To know the meaning of one's name is a powerful thing, particularly when it is a name that can give the person some insight into what might be expected of her in this life. In thinking of baby names myself, it occurred to me that most Americans usually chose names based on how they sound, rather than the African way of choosing a name based on its meaning.

Sobonfu Somé is the author of a wonderful book called *The Spirit of Intimacy*. Born in a remote village of Burkina Faso in West Africa, Somé came to live in Oakland, California, with her husband, author Malidoma Patrice Somé (author of *The Healing Wisdom of Africa*) with the purpose of teaching the ancient wisdom of the tribe throughout the world. From birth, she was aware of her purpose, based on her very name, which means "keeper of ritual" in her native language.

In fact, in her book she explains that it is the belief in her village that "each person chooses her or his life purpose before he or she is even born." Then, when it is time to marry, "our partner, if chosen well, will have been born to a purpose along the same path." If you choose someone who shares your purpose, then you will have a harmonious union. If your partner's purpose is at odds with yours, you are likely to have conflict.

❦ *Partners in Purpose* ❦

Sobonfu and Malidoma (whose name means "be friends with the stranger") are partners in traveling the world to help people—particularly Westerners—find their life purpose through nature, ritual, and community.

When we in the West choose our life partners, we too often do so for the personal reasons of romance. We follow that lustful feeling of passion and interpret that as love. Then, becoming addicted to that "lover's high," we commit ourselves to the person, often marrying, without ever considering our own purpose, much less our partner's, or our common mission as a couple who may contribute children to the world.

I would suggest that we start that all-important dialogue with the person we've fallen in love with by asking, "What are we about as a couple?" What kind of difference do we think we can make in the world together?

I wish my husband and I had had such guidance when we married twenty years ago. We were just groping in the dark for what it would take to have a strong marriage. But blessedly, our intimate conversations in the three years we were together before we married made us realize we shared common goals that translated into our common purpose. It happened, for example, that we met at an event in Harlem which featured Kwame Ture as the keynote speaker, so immediately we knew we shared similar political views. It is doubtful that anyone who didn't believe in black empowerment would have paid money to hear a speech about it.

Those views also extended to our common love of the black community and our joint belief in supporting that community by using the services of black professionals, buying from African American businesses, and working in service to black people.

When couples can find real intimacy, they will realize that it is not just a sexual thing. Real intimacy allows us to share our deep feelings that can help us to follow our passions and our soulfulness. When each partner accepts the other's purpose, and better yet, when they work together to forge a common purpose (in the case of the Somés), the union is all the stronger.

Conflicts occur when there is no meeting of the minds on the mission. If you have a domineering spouse, there is no partnership in purpose. If one person thrives on drama while the other just wants to live in peace, there is a fundamental difference between you that is hard to resolve. Of course, each of us has a unique personality, and opposites do attract, but when one person overpowers and overwhelms the other to the point of squelching that person's spirit, their purpose for being together is also squashed. Acceptance is the key. We may not always agree with those we love, but if we can accept the spirit of who they are, we allow and encourage them to do their life's work.

The same goes for the company you keep. Friends who constantly put you down are not in purpose themselves, so how can they tell you what you should be doing? People whose opinions you trust should have earned that positive influence by showing support; not by telling you "yes" all the time, but by sometimes lovingly turning you in another direction. There's a difference between bullying and guiding. If people are manipulative, they are not in purpose. If people listen and value your judgment, they are. Most important, go by your own gut feelings. If your partner is in sync with you, your spirit will feel it. Your heart will say, "Yeah, I'm feeling you" even when the two of you are too far apart to physically touch.

❤ J-O-B or J-O-Y? ❤

Is your job hard labor or a labor of love? Think of all the hours we spend at work—more time than we spend doing just about anything else.

Since work takes so much of our life, finding work in which we can express our purpose would be ideal.

Unfortunately, so many of us are forced to use work as an "any means necessary" method of survival. Working in a job in which we settle for a paycheck first and satisfaction second (or maybe somewhere farther down the line) is all too common.

To know whether your work is belabored or beloved, pull out your notebook and consider these questions:

- *Does your job serve, benefit, or bless others?* You and your family may benefit from the paycheck, but are the lives of others enhanced by the work you perform? Teachers, coaches, accountants, retail clerks, cashiers, congressmembers, attorneys, CEOs, pilots, Peace Corps workers, Scout leaders, and other people in service jobs all help make our lives better.

- *Do you feel fulfillment on the job, even during stressful times?* Even if you have a difficult job, knowing that it is the right work for you can give you satisfaction that the struggle is worth it. As a magazine editor, I experienced many a hectic, stressful deadline, but knowing that I had a job I loved most of the time helped me get through the stressful times. As health advocate Gary Null advises, when considering our line of work, we should ask ourselves, "What do I feel good doing, that I love doing, that honors me?" Then educate and prepare yourself to be qualified for when the opportunity presents itself to pursue that love.

- *Do you maintain faith in a positive outcome when times are tough?* Financial experts agree that one way to wealth is to own your own business. But those first five years can be a turbulent test of whether a business will succeed. Whether you are starting a business or not, at some point in your life your purpose will be tested. Even in difficult times, if you step out on faith, you are on sure footing.

- *Would you do the job even if you were independently wealthy?* Money can't buy a sense of accomplishment and service to humanity. Jacqueline Kennedy Onassis didn't need to work, but her job as a

book editor brought her a sense of contribution to society and bene-
fited the authors, the company at which she worked, and those who
read the books she edited and published. When you know you are doing the right thing, your inner spirit has an exuberance that keeps on
exclaiming "Yes!"

- *Do you feel as good as you thought you would?* When you are daydreaming, visualizing, planning for your mission, you anticipate that
you will feel good when you are actually doing it. When you do land
that dream job, can you truly say, in the James Brown way "I feel
good! I knew that I would!"? If you can say that on most days, you
probably have found the J-O-Y in your J-O-B.

But what if you are getting no joy from your job? If that is the case,
there are only two things to do: stay or go. If you stay, you take a risk that
you may not have thought of: You risk that your job will always be a vexation to your spirit. That may not seem to be as big a risk as leaving, but
I feel that life is too short to live with a spirit in distress. It usually comes
down to the kind of person you are. Do you fight or flee? Me, I'm outta
there. When the situation does not nourish my spirit, I flee. But if you
are a fighter, it might take you longer to make that decision. You may feel
that you can beat the troubling situation. Sometimes you can. But what
you have to analyze is whether your distress is something that can be
corrected, or if it is a recurring, insidious part of the job. If you have decided that there is no chance that your job will have any redeeming
value in your life, then you are in a bad relationship. Only *you* can say
when it is time to leave a situation that isn't working for you.

Reverend Phyllis E. Crichlow, the minister at Montclair Unity
Church in New Jersey, spoke about this in a sermon. "What do you do
when your work no longer works for you?" she asked the congregation.
"If you are in a bad relationship with your job, and the Voice says,
'Leave,' do you say, 'God, do you have another angel I can talk to?'"

Listen to that inner voice. You may not need to "up and quit" tomorrow, but today you can begin the process of evaluating your skills,
brushing up your résumé, and starting your search for a job that brings
more joy and puts you more in touch with your purpose today. Believe

me, by taking that first step your spirit will begin to feel soothed right away.

❦ *Minds on the Mission* ❦

Patricia A. Johnson, one of my college classmates, has worked in management at the telephone company in San Francisco for the many years since our graduation. Recently she told me that she was back in school, getting her master's degree in telecommunications. After she completes that degree, she said, she wants to get a master's in education so that she can teach either at the junior college level or the third grade. I asked her why she wanted to go back to school after all this time.

"I just feel that our children need good teachers," she replied.

Actually, her succinct answer took considerable, purposeful thought. Single and child-free, she was already comfortable and settled in a home of her own with a nice car. Over the years of good pay and secure benefits at the phone company, she had helped to raise her younger sister and her nephews and nieces. Now, knowing that she would soon have the security of an early-retirement salary, she set out to do the job she *really* wanted to do. By going back to school, she was preparing herself to make a difference.

Helping children was the motivation for a couple of Detroit lawyers, as well. In 1997, Daniel S. Varner and Michael F. Tenbusch chucked their law careers to begin Think Detroit, a nonprofit organization that combines sports leagues and computer classes to help children over age ten acquire computer literacy. Many experts agree that for children who grow up poor, the Internet can expose them to information they might not otherwise have encountered, thereby providing a path to a better future. "We knew the kids needed the character that comes with team sports, and we knew they needed the tools of the future that come with access to technology," Tenbusch was quoted as saying in the *New York Times*. Their program, Balls and Bytes, helps close the gap between technology haves and have-nots by giving children computers donated by area companies. In addition, those children teach older family members the computer skills they've learned.

I don't know if these former attorneys planned for their community efforts to reverberate generationally in that way, but that's the joy of following one's purpose. You never know how far your blessings will flow.

Varner and Tenbusch's case also goes to show that what seems like outward success may not translate to one's inner purpose. Becoming an attorney is quite an accomplishment. Going to law school takes time, money, and hard work. Passing the bar exam is grueling. So, for someone to follow her heart and change course takes courage and vision.

If you are young, you are not going to want to hear this, but I have to say it: You may find that your work life never fulfills you, but that retirement does. That's because we are not our jobs, we are spiritual beings who are driven by what's in our hearts and souls. The demands of paying bills, helping family, and surviving day to day may not allow us the opportunity of having a dream job. But hanging in there with a positive attitude and living a healthy lifestyle that will allow longevity can give you a second chance at a purpose that becomes your life's work, with more meaning than your job.

I admire my mother-in-law, Joyce Oliver, who worked many years as a ground hostess for American Airlines at JFK Airport in New York. She enjoyed meeting the many travelers who passed through the airport and she performed her job well and enjoyed the benefits of free travel. However, her love of serving people grew into volunteer work with greater purpose when she retired from the airline. Having heard about all the HIV/AIDS "border babies" that were abandoned in hospitals in large urban cities that needed nurturing, she volunteered to work in the nursery of the natal unit of a hospital in Queens. Ironically, this was the same hospital in which she had given birth to her children, (including my husband). Joyce had brought children comfortably into the world welcomed by her husband and other family members, yet she decided to try to give other babies to whom she was not related and who had been abandoned by their mothers a chance to start life with love and care. Fortunately now, almost ten years later, there are fewer border babies at that hospital than there used to be, but there are still infants who need holding and babies who need rocking, and Joyce and other caring people are still volunteering, making a difference.

🗝 *Stuck in a Quandary?* 🗝

If you doubt that you will ever decide what your purpose in life is, don't let that make you anxious. Living a righteous life, following a high path, and being in harmony with your own feelings and those of others, will put you in your purpose. That's because we are all here to serve one another. Everything else is just incidentals. Some of us get the sharp vision to see the small print and the details. Others of us stand back and see the big picture. Yet, all in all, the scene is the same.

Even if it seems that right now your purpose eludes you, always remember that no matter who you are, you were created "on purpose for a purpose."

💜 *Your Purpose Journal* * 💜

What is your purpose?

What is your mission in carrying out your purpose?

If you were to put your purpose to music, what song would you play? Is your purpose like jazz, blues, rap, R&B, classical, country, or a little bit rock & roll?

What books reinforce the message of your purpose?

What color is your purpose? (If you close your eyes, what color do you see? What mood do you associate with your purpose?)

What flower represents your purpose?

What Scripture, spiritual passage, or poem magnifies it?

---

*If you don't want to write in this book, make a copy of this page, or take out the notebook, blank book, laptop, PC, or PDA you use for your journal to answer these questions.

$\mathcal{U}$ LTIMACY

Ultimacy—I love that word! And I love a chal-
lenge, which is how the word came to me. At a graduation party, I was
talking with a writer-friend of mine when I mentioned that I was
stumped in trying to start this book. I was having a problem, I explained,
thinking of words to make an acronym for P-U-R-P-O-S-E. "You'd better
change it to S-E-C-R-E-T-S or something else," she advised me, "because you'll never find an inspirational word that starts with a U."

Never? That was all I needed to turn my writer's block into a challenge. I immediately decided to find an inspirational word that started
with a U. Racing home, I couldn't wait to get to my big, fat dictionary to
pour through the Us—and I was quickly rewarded! On the first page of
the letter U, I found this luscious word—ultimacy—which means, as I
briefly discussed in the introduction, simply *the quality or state of being
ultimate*. But the *feeling* of the word—so intimate, so optimum, so ut-
terly utmost—is what did it. Right away, I knew that is how I wanted the
reader to feel while reading this book. I wanted you to have a sense of
ultimacy—of reaching your utmost, your unique potential.

Ultimacy is the intimate relationship with your ultimate self. If we
seek ultimacy, everything else we desire will fall in line. We'll have success, because no one will be better able to do what we do. We'll have
love, because we won't feel the need to depend on others to fulfill us.

We'll have health and happiness, because we will always be willing to pursue our optimum fitness and well-being.

Ultimacy is a new-day way of defining success. It's reaching your utmost, your unique potential. It's what makes you soar from ordinary to extraordinary. The achievement of ultimacy comes from getting to know yourself—and loving what you learn! It's self-motivation that helps you "keep on pushin' in the positive," even when it seems you're the one getting pushed *back*. "Ultimacy" means tapping into the many facets of yourself that can be described by several words starting with the letter "U."

Nine Steps to the Ultimate U

1. BE UNIQUE

There is no one else like you. So why do we all try to be like someone else, to "fit in"? It's our uniqueness that sets us apart and defines our own purpose. Even within the tribe, the team, the community, the church, the job, you can step out on leadership and move the collective purpose forward just by being your unique self. What's a tribe without a chief? What's a sorority without a president? Somebody's got to be in charge—it might as well be you.

When my daughter was born, my husband and I were in a quandary as to what to name her. The name I had called her for nine months in the womb was Alexandra, but when she was born she just didn't look like an Alexandra. Two days after I told the woman in charge of birth certificates that her name would be Alexandra Oliver, we still hadn't announced it to anyone else, and were wondering if we could change it. Finally, I remembered a name my mother had offered, taken from a popular French restaurant she frequented in Seattle, called Annique's. When we mentioned that name to my parents on a coast-to-coast phone call, I could hear my father's enthusiasm, as if he were in the hospital room with us. "Annique—that's *unique!*" And his affirming excitement is the reason we named her Anique, dropping one *n* to make it more like "unique." I figured that if she ever wanted to go into retail, she could hang up a shingle that said "Anique's Unique Antique Boutique." Now a college student, she hasn't expressed any leanings in that direction yet, but she did run for an office at a teen conference once, and we printed up buttons that encouraged kids to vote for "Unique Anique." Although she didn't win, the teens definitely remembered her name. One teen who ran into her several months later said, "I know you, you're Unique Anique!"

Claiming your uniqueness is what can set you apart from the crowd and make you feel special. Being left-handed is an uncommon trait that I like to claim. It's fun to think that you are one of the few people who's in her "right mind." And being African American is special to me. To counter feelings of being a "minority" (a word I have never accepted as an ethnic appellation), I think of being black as being special. Look at it this way: If you are a person of color in a room full of whites, you definitely stand out (but hopefully you won't feel *left* out). Some people are, or would be, uncomfortable in such situations: They don't want to stand out, they want to blend in. But since you can't change the color of your skin, you may as well change your attitude and use the conspicuous attention to your benefit.

In business, if you have a unique product to sell or a unique way to sell it, you'll get more notice. Reading *The Wall Street Journal* recently, I noticed an ad with a full-page photo of an African American man. Of course, this caught my eye, not only because he was handsome, but because it was different and refreshing to see a black broker. The ad piqued my curiosity enough to make me want to read more. I wondered, *What's this brother selling?* Which is exactly what the brokerage firm that placed the ad wanted readers to do—pull me in by the eyeballs.

If you have a unique idea or concept that fills a need, it may turn into a huge success. Jeff Bezos of Seattle thought it might be a good idea to sell books on the Internet—and Amazon.com was born, making a major impact on the bookselling industry and on Internet stocks. Selling books wasn't a new idea, but selling them on the Internet made his concept unique.

You are a "divine original." If you believe that, then you should also know that the success you pursue is yours alone to claim. It's not your mama's, your best friend's, or your man's. It's a goal that is unique to *you*. That's why other people may not always be able to understand it or support it. You've got to believe in it for yourself.

Examples of how someone followed their own dreams, against the will or advice of others are numerous—some are even legendary. When actor Robert Townsend first hit the Hollywood scene he often joked about the uncertainty of the journey it took to get there, saying that his grandmother kept telling him to get a job at the post office.

Mondella Jones can relate. She grew up in Inglewood, California, trying to do all the "right things." After graduating from the University of Southern California in Los Angeles, she took the safe employment road that she says her family encouraged her to do: She became a school teacher. "I had always wanted to do something in publishing," she explained, "but this was a job I knew I could get and that would give me security." Her family was proud of her. She had a respectable, stable job.

What she hadn't planned was the fact that her desire to work in the publishing field would not go away. "I realized after five years of teaching that I had become complacent in my job. And that wasn't good."

Mondella knew in her heart that it would be difficult to excel in her teaching position if she felt indifferent to it. And she also felt that she was not the dedicated teacher her young students deserved. Privately indulging herself in her dream of leaving teaching, she immersed herself in the book world, keeping up with publishing news and taking out a subscription to the trade magazine *Publishers Weekly*.

She also began surfing the Internet, perusing jobs in the book industry. One day Mondella came across a listing for a position at the Howard University Bookstore in Washington, D.C. "I didn't think I would have a chance, living across the country, but I thought, *Why not?* So I applied."

To her surprise, the Howard manager called her right away. Mondella was so delighted to be considered for the job that she paid her own plane fare from Los Angeles to D.C. for the interview. After she flew back, she still didn't know if she had gotten the job or if her risk had been worth it. But after several days of anticipation, she got the word she wanted.

"I didn't know anyone in Washington, D.C.," she says when asked if she had had relatives or friends in the capital. "But I took a chance." At age twenty-seven, she quit an unfulfilling job and moved across the country to start a new career.

Now Mondella's flexibility has paid off again. Moving from Washington, D.C., to New York City, in 2000, she became senior editor of *Black Issues Book Review*. For Mondella, taking her unique path (the Internet) to her own dream (a job in book publishing) brought her a job in which complacency has been replaced by joy.

Someone else's unique desire may have been the opposite: to leave a job at a bookstore to become a teacher. It's not the job itself, it's the passion behind becoming your best ultimate self that's important. And only you can determine that burning desire.

Our family members usually mean well and advise us with good intentions, but when we realize that it's necessary for us to follow a path that others near and dear to us have not trod, it may mean taking that journey alone. The path can be lonely, and you may sometimes, maybe even often, doubt yourself and wonder if you shouldn't have taken their advice. But you have to have faith in yourself and you must always remember the promise of your own uniqueness.

The late Barbara Jordan, the first African American woman elected to the House of Representatives from the South, once said: "I never meant to be a run-of-the-mill person." It's almost impossible to make your mark by pursuing the same path as "everyone else." To be unique, you have to distinguish yourself.

I bet your mother used to say, "If everyone else jumped off a cliff, would you do it, too?" Well, that was some good advice that could be considered in the opposite way: If everyone else just sits on their butts doing nothing, should you do that, too? Well, not if you want to be a success, not if you want to go from ordinary to extraordinary, not if you want to one day stand on a podium at an award show and thank God and your mother.

How to get there: Be different. When everyone else zigs, you zag. Think of what you can do within your work field or your personal life to stand out from others. If you want to attract and keep love, for example, be unique in your approach. Do something totally original, or absolutely unexpected. Use your imagination and go for it.

I often visualize the unique path one has to take in this way: You are driving down the freeway of success. There are many cars on this highway; in fact, it's like nonstop rush hour. You move over to the fast lane. You're passing people in other lanes, and it feels good. You're accelerating, moving fast, pedal to the metal. At some point, however, you realize you've got to get off at your exit. No one else seems to be getting off. Cars in the other lanes don't slow down or let you in. You've got to do it yourself. You've got to put on your blinker, watch the traffic, move cautiously—all the while making sure that you make it to the right exit. The traffic continues at the same fast pace up the highway, but *you* must take the right path to your own destination.

At work, be original in your ideas. Think "outside the box." Don't be afraid to say what you think. If you don't say what you're thinking, someone else may. Or, if you hold back, the world may never have the benefit of your contributions. As the old adage goes, nothing ventured, nothing gained.

2. TRY THE UNEXPECTED

Terrie Williams, founder of the Terrie Williams Agency in New York, is known for sending brief handwritten notes to friends and business acquaintances. I felt blessed to receive one of them once when I was in the middle of a sticky job transition. "I know this is a difficult time for you," her note read, "but hang in there. I'm thinking of you." It may have taken her only a few minutes to write the note and address it, but knowing Terrie's nonstop schedule as head of her own public relations firm, I also knew just how precious her time was, and I was grateful that she took time out for me. Terrie's unexpected notes are a successful business strategy that help people she's just met remember her, and also keeps her in touch with friends she doesn't see often. I often tell Terrie that I want to be just like her when I grow up.

Doing the unexpected always gets points, especially if you do something beyond your job or personal responsibilities. From teenagers tak-

ing the initiative to help with housework to adults taking on more duties in the workplace, unexpected efforts are often an easy way to be recognized.

How to get there: Surprise loved ones. Do something unanticipated for
your boss. Show up to volunteer at a retirement home or go to a hospital
and hold a "border baby." Your gesture will be appreciated, guaranteed.

3. BE UNEQUALED

When you do whatever you do better than anyone else, you'll always get
ahead. Ask Dr. Benjamin Carson, the director of pediatric neurosurgery
at Johns Hopkins Medical Center in Baltimore. Known internationally
for performing the delicate and intricate brain surgery required to separate German conjoined twins who were joined at the head in the late
1980s, he's still making headlines for such life-and-death operations.
More recently, Dr. Carson successfully removed half of the brain of a
fifteen-year-old girl to prevent the spread of a rare and deadly disease
that causes seizures and eats away brain tissue. Do you think anyone
holds his brown skin against him when they need someone to save their
life? It's hard (and ignorant) to be prejudiced in a life-threatening situation. People want the best, someone who's unequaled in his or her ability to do the job. You know how people always discount how hard
something is by saying "It's not like it's rocket science or brain surgery"?
I read a story about Dr. Carson in the February 1998 issue of *Fast Company* magazine titled, "This Is Brain Surgery." Because Dr. Carson is unequaled in his skill as a neurosurgeon, he is admired and revered. Go
follow his lead and be the best at whatever you do. Olympic athletes
know that what is required to win is to be unequaled. That's how Marion
Jones, Jackie Joyner-Kersee, Lisa Leslie, and Muhammad Ali have made
history.

For centuries, African Americans have fought hard to just be regarded as equal to white Americans. As an additional demand, many of
us were raised to believe that to prove ourselves we have to do a job
twice as well as nonblacks to be considered "just as good." It's not fair,
but until the playing field is even, that's still the strategy to success.

How to get there: To be unequaled in your field, begin with a clear desire to be the best. Then follow up with the preparation, the education, and the dedication to the task. Study the competition to see how they reached their goals. Then outdo them in a work environment; make those with the decision-making power feel that "nobody does it better" than you do. You want people to think, *Well, we've tried the rest, now we've got to get the best!* And that means *you.*

4. GO FOR THE UNUSUAL

Sarah Greaves-Gabaddon was in her twenties and working as a publicity professional at Sandals beach resort in Jamaica when she decided she wanted to try something new. She had long wanted to see what it would be like to live in New York City, so after she met me and my family when we were on vacation in Jamaica, she volunteered to work as an intern at *Heart & Soul* magazine, where I was the editor-in-chief. I knew that she was really overqualified for that job, but since she was so passionate about her plan to live in New York and work at a magazine, I felt lucky to get such a high-quality employee. It all worked out for the benefit of both Sarah and *Heart & Soul.* However, being such a go-getter made her irreplaceable at Sandals, and in no time her boss wooed her back—with plenty of incentives—cutting her sabbatical short. So her surprise move to New York paid off in unexpected ways.

It also doesn't hurt to *be* something different. I remember an executive secretary at *Essence* many years ago who was highly proficient at her job, but a bit quirky. She often said funny things or had an unusual take on a situation. We laughed a lot around her and she enjoyed amusing people. One day another staffer said to me, "That woman is something different!" Her unusual approach to life made her memorable and well liked among just about everyone she met.

How to get there: Pull yourself away from the ordinary by doing something extraordinary. Here's a role model for you: Oseola McCarty. It's unusual for a domestic worker to give thousands of dollars to a college to ensure that students would get the educational opportunities that she did not have, but that's exactly what the late Ms. McCarty of Hattiesburg, Mississippi, did in 1995 when she donated $150,000 of her life savings to endow a scholarship fund for poor students at the University of Southern Mississippi—a school in her hometown that she had never even visited. Having worked as a washerwoman since age twelve to earn money to care for a sick aunt, at age eighty-seven McCarty gave the gift that brought her national attention, including a Presidential Citizens Award from President Clinton. An eighteen-year-old Hattiesburg High School honors graduate, Stephanie Bullock, became the first to benefit from that extraordinary act of generosity, determination, and compassion. And the rest of the nation was awed by McCarty's actions. Even CNN founder and multibillionaire, Ted Turner, expressed his admiration for this elderly woman who made her small fortune a few dollars at a time. After hearing of McCarty's generosity, in 1997 he promised to give $1 billion to support the United Nations. This gift is perhaps the largest single donation by a private individual in history. "If that little woman can give away everything she has," he said, "then I can give a billion."

If you don't donate money on a regular basis, do something unusual and give a small amount of money to a charity. Arthur Mitchell, the founder, president, and artistic director of the Dance Theatre of Harlem, told me in an interview for *Essence* several years ago that when his company was once in financial difficulty, it was the help of everyday people in the community who sent in five or ten dollars that really did help offset the deficit and boost the dance company's spirits until a substantial gift from American Express came through. "Everyone thinks, 'I don't have a million dollars,'" he said. "But we've got supporters on welfare and people who are widows. And they say, 'My check is not so much this week, Mr. Mitchell, but here's five dollars.'"

5. HAVE A SENSE OF URGENCY

People who live like there may not be a tomorrow, or that there may not be a second chance, often excel because of their sense of urgency. Young achievers often feel the rush to get to the next level fast, and they do their jobs with seriousness and a set plan.

What often makes the difference is setting goals to have a certain task accomplished by a particular date or age. Take Jackie Lewis, for example. Living in Brooklyn in the early seventies, she decided that she wanted to own her own business and her own home by the time she was thirty years old. Her sense of urgency and focus propelled her to accomplish those very goals by the timetable she had set. When I interviewed her for *Essence,* she had indeed opened a lovely antique-clothing store in the SoHo area of Manhattan that not only made her one of the youngest proprietors around but also a trendsetter who encouraged young, avant-garde people to make that neighborhood a popular place. Her success allowed her to buy a spacious brownstone in the Fort Greene section of Brooklyn, a neighborhood that later became known for being the home of Spike Lee and Chris Rock. And she did it all by age thirty.

How did she follow that act? Being a woman who had always marched to the beat of her own drummer, Jackie eventually followed a reggae beat, selling her boutique, Le Grand Hotel, and trading it for a more peaceful and spiritual life in Jamaica. Again she epitomized the unique trendsetter with a sense of urgency. Jackie is one of the few black women in the world to embrace the concept of resort-spa ownership. Opened in 1993, "Jackie's on the Reef" in Negril, Jamaica, is now well known among spa-addicted women like me.

"I felt I had accomplished a great deal in my life," Jackie told me, "but I still wasn't happy. So I went to Jamaica, where I had always gone to get away from New York. Then I decided to build a holistic spa where people could come to work on themselves, like I was doing."

Being an early bloomer allowed Jackie not only the chance to enjoy success while she was still young, but to reward herself with a more laid-back second career. Her sense of urgency gave birth to a sense of peace and freedom—it wasn't an end unto itself. It was one tactic, among others.

How to get there: You can tap into your own sense of urgency by setting timetables for goals, and plotting out the steps to get there. How long does it normally take to accomplish what you want to do? Next, figure out what you can do to accelerate the process without compromising the quality of work.

In fact, the mission should be to do it thoroughly, as well as rapidly. If in your effort to get things done quickly you skirt over the details or don't get the job done well, you'll lose out. Too many people confuse a sense of urgency with "getting over." Don't do just enough to get by. Do what it takes to do the task well.

In her speeches, Children's Defense Fund president Marian Wright Edelman chides young people who think they can take the elevator to success; climbing the ladder step by step is still the most effective way to "pay your dues" and gain the respect of your supervisors, colleagues, and subordinates. And do it with integrity and high ethics. Endeavor to cover every important aspect of your project. You can still have a sense of urgency while sitting back to examine and evaluate your progress from time to time.

6. Stay Unbought and Unbossed

Shirley Chisholm, the first African American woman to serve in the United States Congress, called her autobiography *Unbought and Unbossed*. The title reflected her pride in being her own woman; no one could buy her integrity or convince her to vote against her conscience. That strong will propelled her to declare her candidacy for the 1972 Democratic presidential nomination—making history again. More recently, in 2000, another Democrat, Jon Corzine of New Jersey, borrowed the "unbought and unbossed" slogan for his own bid for the U.S. Senate.

Being "unbought" is a matter of integrity. It means that you are your own person, that no one has paid or bribed you to act or speak in a particular way. An unbought person is a free thinker, an independent spirit. One who is "unbossed" is a leader, even when others demand she be a follower. I think of Winnie Madikizela-Mandela as a person who remained unbought and unbossed throughout her struggle to be free under South Africa's apartheid system of oppression. She was a fierce opponent to the forces that sought to break her and boss her. White supremacists may have believed they should have owned her, and they separated her from her children, putting her in solitary confinement for months to try to do so, but she couldn't be bought. Under apartheid, it was common for blacks to refer to the domineering whites as "boss" or "boss man," but the truth has now prevailed. I don't think anyone would expect Nelson Mandela or his successor as president, Thabo Mbeke, to call anyone "boss." Because South African blacks remained unbought and unbossed in their collective souls, they won the revolution for freedom.

How to get there: Is there a situation in which you find yourself bucking the system? If you know deep in your heart what the high moral ground is, even though it goes against the grain of some bullying forces in your life, hold on tight to your beliefs. Think about people in history or our culture that you admire for standing up for what they believe. Examine how this stance differs from stubbornness or arrogance. Study the ethics of each circumstance you find yourself in. Then go in the direction that takes you higher without compromising your integrity.

7. BE ULTRACOOL

Haki Madhubuti once wrote a poem that describes a brother so cool, they call him Refrigerator. There's something to be said about cool people.

If you are cool, you're slow to anger, you know how to "go with the flow," you're calm and centered. That's not to say that it's easy, although some people probably "got it that way" more naturally than others. It often takes premeditation.

One day I heard some yelling and loud talking outside my house. When I looked outside I saw about four or five workmen in the back of a pickup truck. One was yelling to someone in the cab of the truck, "Well you should know! You're the f—ing supervisor! You're supposed to know these m—-f—ing things!" He was definitely not cool. Too often, we don't stop to think whether our reaction is really overreaction, or if we end up responding in a more inflammatory way than the offense. And when we do act out, we do so before thinking of what the consequence of our actions may be, like being viewed as having an "attitude problem," or being held back from promotions.

Sometimes it's not easy to be cool when you feel you are being threatened. During the civil rights movement, nonviolent protesters often had to be coached on how to react without responding in the way they would normally—say, by arguing back or punching somebody in the mouth. Some men felt that to not respond with force marginalized their manhood. But nonviolence is a mind game. It's a tactic. A strategy to outwit your opponent. It's mind over manhood—or womanhood—in favor of humanhood. And it's not just an old sixties concept.

Can you be too cool? I'm sure some people would say so. No one wants to be perceived as a wimp. But if you are ultracool, you're not square, you're not a wimp. You are strong and calm under pressure.

How to get there: Are you a cool cat? Or a hothead? If you are a parent, you probably have read about how to count to ten when you are angry with your child. To avoid "going off," experts say it's best to wait a while to address a volatile situation.

That's also good advice when confronting an adult. Mad at your spouse, significant other, or best friend? Be cool. Collect your thoughts and your emotions. Plot out a strategy for discussing the situation. Have a resolution in mind. You just may find it to be more satisfying, and more productive, than a blow out.

Meditation can also help a hot temper. When one is in a habit of stepping away from stress each day, one can better cope when confronted by a provocation. Calm becomes the comfort zone one chooses over conflict.

8. Seek the Ultimate

It's the basis of ultimacy to seek the ultimate. Strive for the best, put yourself to the test. Push it to the max. I mean push your abilities, but don't burn yourself out. We need you!

When I was twenty-one, I had a job interview for a summer internship with a very important woman in publishing, Mary Campbell, the secretary of the Condé Nast Publications. She asked me the most common question interviewers ask: "What would you like to be doing in five years?" That was easy. "I'd like to be editor-in-chief of a national women's magazine." Here I was, a little colored girl (seated in front of her with cornrows, no less), saying that I wanted to run a magazine like those her company published—which happened to be *Vogue, Mademoiselle, Glamour, Bride's,* and *House & Garden.* In 1973, hardly ten years after lunch-counter sit-ins in the South, it wouldn't have been so "politically incorrect" if she had had a good laugh and shooed me out of her office. But instead, I think she responded to my earnestness and ambition, and saw those traits as an indication that I might work hard toward my goal. Shooting for the ultimate, I got the job. And ultimately, I did become editor-in-chief of the national women's magazine *Heart & Soul.*

What's your ultimate ambition? Don't let it intimidate you. Believe in it. Think *someone has to do it.* Someone has to fill that open position you saw in that classified ad. Someone has to be principal of that elementary school. Someone has to own the most popular beauty salon in town. It might as well be you.

How to get there: Do what you can to prepare yourself for your ultimate dream. There's a saying that success happens when preparation meets opportunity.

Obsess about your dream. Read and study all you can to become an expert in your area of interest. My sister-friend's son, Charlie, loves cars. As a little child, he talked about cars, drew pictures of cars, and could point out any model on the street. Now that he's a teenager he buys European car magazines, and if any of his family or friends are considering buying an automobile, he's the first one they consult. Charlie's a walking, talking *Consumer Reports* on car performance and reliability. In following his passion, he is preparing himself for an ultimate career in the high-paying engineering or design fields. And if he chooses not to go that route, he will at least know what rewards steeping oneself in an avocation can bring.

9. BE UNDETERRED

Another word for "undeterred" is "persistence"—to continue on resolutely in spite of difficulties. Couple that with "tenacity"—to hold fast.

I have learned that the secret to every success I have ever had has been persistence. In my experience, nothing ever comes *easily.* It takes persistence, follow-up, continuing on undeterred.

When *Glamour* magazine held its 30th anniversary of their Top Ten College Contest, I was invited to attend the shindig at the renowned Four Seasons restaurant in New York City. I hadn't really been a "top ten" winner. Let's say I was a "top fifteen" because officially, I had been named an honorable mention winner of the contest. But as years went by and I had been an editor at *Glamour* and at *Essence,* and I had became a "favorite daughter" of sorts, *Glamour* "upgraded" me by referring to me as winner in promotional material and even in the magazine. Not wanting to "front," I tried to set the record straight when I was invited to the anniversary (knowing I'd be the only also-ran there) and I was told, "Well you should have been a winner. So we'll just say you were one." And with that, the history of it was deconstructed—fortunately for me.

In the video made for the anniversary, the longtime, legendary editor of the magazine, Ruth Whitney, had the task of identifying the characteristics that made each woman present a winner. To my surprise, she said, "The thing I remember most about Stephanie is that she was persistent."

About ten years later, I sadly attended Mrs. Whitney's memorial service. Like many such occasions, it turned out to be a bittersweet reunion. Past and present *Glamour* magazine colleagues mingled at a reception after the tribute at which Katie Couric, of the *Today* show, spoke movingly, along with *Ms.* magazine editor Marcia Anne Gillespie (who hired me away from *Glamour* when she was editor-in-chief of *Essence),* and former college winner Sheryl Lee Ralph, now an actress. Greeting an acquaintance that I hadn't seen in quite a while, I reminded her of who I was and she said, "I remember you. You're the one Ruth said was so persistent."

I wasn't sure if that sounded like a compliment or something closer to a "pest," but I decided to accept it as the former, mainly because I had to admit that it was true. When I was in Seattle, home from college attending a *Mademoiselle* magazine event, I decided that I'd like to have a job like the editors that I had met there. It might have seemed like an unlikely ambition. But being young and ambitious, I never thought that way. I just kept taking step after step to make my dream a reality.

First, I asked one of the *Mademoiselle* editors at the event how she got her job. She said she had been a *Mademoiselle* representative at her college, and she told me to look for the application form in the upcoming issue of the magazine. I did exactly what she advised. Then, as a rep, I made friends with the editors who administered the college rep board. I persistently asked them how I could get a job there. They told me who to talk to. It was the aforementioned Mary Campbell, and I persisted in calling her to get an appointment for an interview. After I succeeded in that endeavor and served as a summer intern, I kept in touch with Ms. Campbell while I was finishing my senior year of college. Then, to try to create some buzz around myself, hoping to ensure that the company would remember me and offer me a job upon graduation, I entered the *Glamour*'s Top Ten College Contest. My honorable mention got me pictured in the back of the magazine, not the cover like my friend Kate White, who is now the editor-in-chief of *Cosmopolitan*. It didn't even get me that year's "token black girl" spot—that went to Erlene Berry Wilson—who is now one of my closest friends. But it did land me a job as junior editor. And that was fine with me. I was the only African American editor at *Glamour* at the time, until Erlene joined the team. Looking back, I guess I *was* persistent. But at the time, I did whatever I needed to do to get the job—I guess you could say I got the job "by any means necessary."

In later years, I recognized and admired the persistence of several of the young sisters I hired at *Essence*. I fondly recall one in particular. Curtia James worked in book publishing, but she wanted to make the switch to magazines. She contacted *Essence,* seeking a job as an editorial assistant, but there were no openings. So she decided to write freelance articles for my section of the magazine, "Contemporary Living." Soon I began to notice that quite frequently when Curtia would talk with me, she would ask, "Have any job openings yet?" In addition, when she would turn in her assignments, she would also enclose a résumé with a note reminding me that the next time there was a job available she would like to be considered. Well, Curtia was so persistent that it was not only apparent that she wanted the job, but that if she were ever hired, she would be just as tenacious about her work. Sure enough, a position became available, and we called Curtia to interview for it. We never called or even considered another candidate. She got the job— and she did it well.

How to get there: As the Gospel song says, "Hold out just a little while longer!" Unless the person in power who makes the decisions actually tells you no, why give up? When you call or write someone and they don't respond right away, that's no reason to stop trying. Call again. Write again—and again. Send an e-mail next time. Follow up with a fax. Undeterred, you just might end up with your desire.

AND ONE TO GROW ON: KNOW YOU'RE "THE BOMB"

Don't misunderstand me, "the bomb" is not to be confused with "a bomb." We've got to get our word play together here. A bomb is a dud. I don't want you to bomb; I want you to be "the bomb," explosive, in that fireworks kind of way. Glorious, colorful, full of wonderment and joy. Being the bomb is a way of signifying the best, what's exciting, what's the ultimate.

A lot of men think Tyra Banks is the bomb. Jennifer Lopez, Janet Jackson, and Vanessa Williams are the bomb. Actually, in that context, the phrase is closer to "bombshell."

How to get there: Let's see, how did Tyra Banks get there? She tried out for modeling, even though she had been teased as a child for being so tall and skinny. How did Jennifer Lopez do it? Her self-confidence with her body prompted *People* magazine to call her the Queen of Curves. How did Janet Jackson get there? She broke away from the shadow of her famous brothers and took "control" of her own destiny. How did Vanessa Williams become the bomb? After her stint as Miss America literally bombed, she kept her head up and her dreams alive, and made one of the most triumphant comebacks of anyone in the public eye.

How do *you* become a success? Do what they did: Believe in yourself in spite of what people say about you. Break away from the family business—even if it's successful, there's another kind of achievement you have in mind. And like Vanessa, even if you fail or have a setback, keep your head high and continue to work toward your dream.

🎗 Tiny Tips for Getting to the Top 🎗

There are many little things that people can do to get ahead. And when I say "get ahead," I mean break out from the crowd, move your life forward. Like Arthur Mitchell said, people think they have to do big things to make a difference, but it's the consistent accumulation of small things and details that often characterize one's success. For example:

FOLLOW THROUGH

I once heard a motivational speaker start a speech to a group of teenagers with this teaser: If five birds are sitting in a tree limb and one decides to fly away, how many are left? [Did I hear you say four?] Answer: Five, because one only *decided*—he didn't fly away, he only decided to.

So, don't just decide that you are unique. *Do* something that sets you apart from the crowd. Follow through.

FINISH WHAT YOU START

So many of us have good intentions, but we just let things fall between the cracks. If you say you're going to do something, try your best to deliver. If you see that you can't deliver, at least notify the people who will be affected or who may be anticipating your action. It sounds like common sense to say that we should finish what we start, but it's not always common practice. Make sure that people know they can rely on you.

Recently, I asked a computer consultant to come to my house to advise me on how to increase the memory of my hard drive so I could upgrade my Internet service. He came over right away, but had to leave before he had completed the task. Saying he'd return that afternoon, he went off to another appointment. He didn't return that day, or the next, or the next week, or the next month. I called and left *mucho* messages— still no return call, no explanation, not a peep. Fortunately, I figured out how to use the Internet myself and I got around his incomplete job. But as far as he knows, I'm still incapacitated and waiting for him to finish the job. In addition, he penalized himself, because he couldn't bill me for a job he hadn't completed. So he denied himself payment. I certainly hope that my experience with his not finishing what he started was an exception to the way he normally works. But since the computer consultant didn't finish what he started, I know I did not see his ultimate, best self.

GIVE CLOSURE

Don't leave people hanging. In my job as a magazine editor, I have had to deal with tons of celebrities. Some have layers and layers of staff people one has to wade through in order to connect with them. Others respond right away, telling you yes or no, cutting to the chase. Those are usually the ones who are the most successful.

I always tell people that Bill Cosby and Nikki Giovanni are two people who are longtime, successful public figures because they take care of business in a timely fashion. Each time I have ever had reason to call either of them with an interview request, I have received an answer in time to take the next step effectively. That's not to say that they have always said yes, but even if the answer has been no, by responding quickly, they enabled me to regroup and interview someone else. But people who are trifling about getting back to others just belabor the process and drag out the situation. And by the time one does respond after taking *forever,* the person making the request has a negative opinion of the person. And if she doesn't have the courtesy to respond at all, the person asking may not only have negative vibes toward her, she may get mad. Then that vibe multiplies because she'll most likely tell other people about the bad experience she had with the person who just didn't take the time to extend the courtesy of a reply.

Of course, things do happen: Mail gets lost, faxes don't go through, people procrastinate in order not to reject others. But like an item I once read in *Writer's Digest* said, people can deal with rejection easier than nonresponse. If someone sends a query letter to a magazine asking if an editor might be interested in a story idea, the writer would rather have a quick "no, thanks" than no reply at all. In the time the writer takes to worry and fret about when an editor will respond, the writer could brush off the rejection and send the story elsewhere. So just tell someone if their idea works for you or not, and bring closure for both of you, whether your response is positive or negative. If it doesn't work for you, it may work for someone else, and everything will still turn out okay for all parties involved.

🖤 Have a "Goal Model" 🖤

After so much talk about celebs who object to being "role models," such as basketball players Dennis Rodman and Charles Barkley, versus good sports like Michael Jordan (who bears the burden graciously) and WNBA star Lisa Leslie ("I love being a role model for little girls!"), I was a bit tired of that phrase, "role models." It's been totally played out. And it always seemed that it was black folks who were expected by the media to need and or be role models. I mean, I never recall hearing any other folks being asked who their role models were, or being questioned about being a good role model. Has anyone ever asked Howard Stern or Courtney Love if they consider themselves positive role models for young people?

Author Debrena Jackson Gandy put a new spin on this subject for me. I once heard her call publicist Teresa Lyles Holmes her "goal model." "Teresa is my goal model because she juggles her career and her marriage and mothering of three children so well," Debrena said when she became acquainted with Teresa at the African American Women on Tour conference. Debrena has three young children herself, as well as a husband and a busy career as a writer and motivational speaker.

Having a goal model makes you take the initiative in mapping out your road to success, first by defining your goal, then by identifying someone whose successes you can emulate. Authors Iyanla Vanzant, Sarah Ban Breathnach, Deepak Chopra, and others are goal models for me on my road to finding my ultimate place in the writing world. My husband says I am "studying success." I read everything about my goal models I can get my hands on. I think of how I can apply their strategies to myself. I analyze what worked for them and what might work for me. It's a lot like being a fan of the person, except it's with a purpose— to seek your own success. Fawning all over someone, being a fanatic (the word from which "fan" derives its root), has no purpose except to make yourself feel a false familiarity with a person you do not even know.

As so many celebrities have said, including Michael Jordan and Bill Cosby, the best role models are our own parents. If you had a mother or a father (or both!), for example, who worked hard to provide for your family, then they're great role models of how to persevere, be strong, and succeed against adversity. Maybe an aunt, uncle, or grandparent has had a great impact on your life. Sometimes we forget how those who are closest to us have affected our lives.

James P. Comer, M.D., recounts in his 1988 book *Maggie's American Dream: The Life and Times of a Black Family* that his mother (after whom the book is named) was a "hard taskmaster" and that for years he held feelings of "anger and resentment that she had pushed me so hard." But with maturity, his feelings gave way to admiration for this woman, who believed that education was the way to opportunity. Although she had been denied that opportunity herself, a lack of education and low income did not stop her and her husband from giving all five of their children the support needed to acquire thirteen college degrees. Now Dr. Comer himself provides support in the field of education. As the Maurice Falk Professor of Child Psychiatry at the Yale University School of Medicine's Child Study Center, Comer is nationally known for his innovative programs to improve inner-city schools. With his mother as a role model, he has taken her goals to another level—that of helping *many* low-income children achieve the opportunity that a quality education brings.

THE ROLE VERSUS THE GOAL

The difference between having role models and goal models is that the latter provides you with a more specific road map for reaching your goals. The trick is to identify people who have achieved success *in the way that you would like to.* It doesn't mean you have to cultivate a relationship with those people, as you would with a mentor; it just means that you follow the pattern they used to achieve their success in order to plot out your own.

Pull out your journal and make a list of the goal models in your own life. Who are they? Think of what you admire about them, and how they influence you.

Be U

Sammy Davis, Jr., had a big hit called "I've Got to Be Me." His Rat Pack buddy, Frank Sinatra, had one called "My Way." Both point to the challenge of being an individual, of realizing who you are, and then acting on it.

As a teenager in Seattle, I liked to wear black. Who knows why? I thought it was cool. I suppose because Seattle's reputation for gray weather, drab-color clothes were not necessarily part of the cultural landscape back then. In other words, I was definitely the only one who wore a black dress (albeit with a white ruffled neckline) to my junior prom. But I was being me.

Sometimes, you can find that elsewhere in the world others share your sense of individuality. When I moved to New York City after college, I felt right at home in the sea of women and men dressed in black. Be yourself, and somewhere out there you just may find your comfort zone.

🖤 Join the Uprising 🖤

It started as a germ of an idea I had: Diversify this book. I thought I would add the point of view of someone on the spiritual path who is not black. Marianne Williamson, a Jewish minister of a Unity church in Detroit and author of bestsellers including *A Return to Love,* was featured in The Learning Annex catalog I got in the mail. When I was at *Essence,* I had heard of her from coworkers who enjoyed her books and attended her lectures. So I decided to enroll in one of her courses, billed as "A Spiritually Healing and Transformational Evening." The catalog copy further stated in boldface type: "**Marianne's innovative, creative, and inspiring ideas will let you design personal goals that will help transform you and your world!**"

I didn't think I needed any transforming—I was doing pretty well, thank you. I just needed to take some notes so that I could write up an interesting little passage for this book. But whoa, was I in for a surprise! By the time I left the Community Church in New York City, where the lecture was held, I did, indeed, feel that I had been spiritually healed and transformed. I learned that you don't have to think you *need* transformation to be transformed!

Arriving alone and late to the full sanctuary of several hundred people, I sat down in the back and noticed the racial diversity. Marianne was saying something that caught my attention: "There's a collective spiritual uprising happening."

She continued with a discussion about "the pool of spiritual power": "Martin Luther King, Jr., said we have a power within us more powerful than bullets. Moving mountains is small compared to what we can do with prayer and meditation. When Jesus meditated then spoke, mountains moved, Lazarus rose. Try this exercise: Go into meditation—a space of nonviolent power within us—then speak."

I took notes as she finished her lecture and went on to have an exchange with the audience. Here are some of the questions they asked and she answered:

Question: *I am jealous of people, like you, who are doing something they love. How can I have patience in finding what I am here to do?*

Marianne: We all have the same job here: We are all ministers of God. You can't find what you have to *do* because you haven't found who you *are* yet. You don't need the Holy Spirit to tell you what to do, but you do need to unblock your heart. Ask Him to heal your heart and make you a miracle of God. When you know Who is inside you, the person outside will find you a job you love. In the meantime, it keeps you humble to know you're not doing that well on every issue. [Laughter from the audience.]

Question: *How can I live again after losing at love?*

Marianne: Everyone has a story of love lost. This is a particularly potent issue for women. You create what you defend. We say, "I can't trust this guy," then we go into a defensive posture. We get defensive when we don't need to be, or we're too open.

We have choices to [either] shut down or to open up wider. Most folks feel if you open up, you will get hurt; If you don't open up, you won't get hurt again. Some people move into a zone of: "I've been hurt so much that I cannot bear to be hurt anymore." If there is an area of hurt left, there will be someone to hurt you.

Let us pray for the bruises of our heart: We ask that the Spirit enter us and make us whole. We ask for forgiveness for those who have hurt us, for those we hold grievances against. Amen.

[A man in the audience stood up to say: "Pain is inevitable. Suffering is optional."]

Question: *What is a holy relationship?*

Marianne: There has to be a transition from a "special" relationship to holy. That is one in which we concentrate on forgiveness, not control. Deep romantic relationships are an "inquiry." Holiness is where we realize we are together to heal together, that the relationship is a temple of healing. Our capacity goes deep to hurt each other—and to heal each other. Two people can live together without much going on but politeness. But the couple that prays together stays together.

Then a young white man asked Marianne a question that struck a chord with me, and it pointed to what our country needs to address in order to find its purpose and mind its collective mission.

Question: *If we have affirmative action, why do we need reparations?*

Marianne: If someone takes my television, then calls me and says, "Hey, I got it," I'm going to say, "I want it back!"

There needs to be an apology for slavery. The Pope said, "Until we do, we'll be asleep to today's problems." Until we apologize about slavery, we can also lie about other abuses that happen today.

Nothing is more of a threat than a passionate-thinking woman, because such women give birth to passionate-thinking children. Take race relations in this country. Slavery was not the problem, racism was. The stroke of the pen in the Emancipation Proclamation did not eradicate that. That is our generation's job to do.

We are just beginning to see that reparations is not an outrageous concept, but rather, now in our spiritual perception of growth, it is necessary.

What would we pay? Think of the unpaid labor of the South. The North won the war, so we owe the debt: $100 billion.

We have to have affirmative action long enough to have our consciousness changed. Moses had to wander forty years for the consciousness to be changed. There is a wrong that needs to get right. There's a difference between taking blame and taking responsibility. Why is there such resistance?

The economy of the United States is the legacy of slavery. That's a historical fact. So why are we resistant to [acknowledging] a debt that needs to be paid? We spend money on the military industrial complex, but what scares you [white people] more? China [becoming a world trade power] or walking through Harlem?

African Americans have a lot of unexpressed things to say. So we [whites] are afraid to have a conversation because people [whites] are afraid they'll [blacks will] get emotional.

Shall we do the Prayer of Atonement?

I admit that I didn't know what that was. I hadn't read any of Marianne Williamson's books or listened to any tapes or ever heard her speak before. So, I was pretty stunned when she went on to say, "Will everyone in the room who is African American please stand up?" That meant me!

Putting down my notepad and quickly feeling self-conscious, I noticed about twenty other black folks standing, scattered throughout the sanctuary that was filled with a couple hundred people.

"Now, will anyone who is white, who is near them, please take a hand of each African American, so that both their hands are held?" Two women, one in the row behind me, who looked to be in her thirties, with whom I had been chatting during the break, and the other, an older, stylish woman who had been sitting two seats down from me, stood up to take my hands. "I ask the white people to repeat after me," Marianne said, and she began slowly and deliberately to recite the prayer "Amends to the African American," which is published in her bestselling book *Illuminata*, pausing line by line:

For what has been done to hurt you and offend you,
For the evils of racism throughout our history,
Please forgive me and please forgive this country.
I acknowledge to you the evils that have occurred here
In your life and in the lives of your ancestors.
On behalf of my nation, I deeply apologize.
If I could rewrite history I would, but I cannot.
God can. Dear God, please do.
I acknowledge now the genius of your people,
And the brilliance of your spirit,
And the pain you have endured.
May the demon of racism be cast off,
Out of this country and away from this world,
May there be in this nation a correction and resurrection,
That nevermore shall any hearts be enslaved.
May the future be made new.
May the pain of the past be gone forever.
May past hatred, dear God, now become a present love.
May forgiveness truly wash us clean.
May black and white America have a miraculous healing.
May we begin again as brothers, for that is what we are.
God bless your children unto all generations.
May the spirit of this amends bring peace to your soul.
Truly, you have waited long.
I bless your children.
Please bless mine.
I thank you.
And I thank God.
Amen.

This was an unexpectedly emotional moment for me. I hadn't in my wildest imagination expected Marianne to go *there*. And I hadn't gone to this lecture with any burdens to soothe. There were no personal past hurts from lovers or childhood abuses I was harboring. There was no lack of purpose in my work, and no estranged relationships in my family.

Although I am always looking for higher spiritual ground, I didn't feel that I had any pent-up angst or resentments.

I had been an activist for civil rights in the 1960s and remained passionate about injustice, but I had never in my forty-eight years allowed myself to dwell in the rage of racism. However, as Marianne spoke, I looked in the eyes of the women holding my hands and they each returned my gaze with a depth I rarely experienced with white people. This disarmed me because they seemed entirely sincere about the words they repeated, as though they weren't just mouthing the words because they had been put on the spot; that maybe they actually needed to say this.

Yet, I had never realized how much I had needed an apology. I hadn't allowed myself to feel the hurt I had buried within me about racism. How could I? There was no outlet for that. African Americans learn to be strong, to be hard. Our parents and our community teach us to throw up an armor around our feelings. For many of us that translates into an anger or bitterness that is constantly being pushed under the surface so that we can survive as a "minority" in a country that does not value us.

No white person had ever told me they were sorry. No white person had apologized for the barrage of vexations to the spirit that were so common they were almost stereotypical; just the day before, after I had bought a ticket to this very lecture, a taxi passed me right by as I stood soaked in the pouring rain, my arm frantically waving, only to pick up a young white guy on Fifth Avenue a few feet from me. No one had ever said they were sorry for the constant, subtle racial insults that accumulate deep in your soul over a lifetime. No one had ever apologized for the day that I went to work at *Vogue* in the morning, only to be jolted back to racist reality that night when another white person thought nothing of slamming the door in my face in Brooklyn Heights when I went to view an apartment for rent. "We don't want any blacks or Puerto Ricans," the woman had had the arrogance to say through the bars of the stately brownstone's basement door. It was hard to believe this was the same person who had spoken so nicely on the phone to me that afternoon—when, I assume, she thought the *Vogue* staffer was white.

Sadly, my personal racial slights pale in comparison to the anxiety black folks in general live with, such as the fear of racial profiling; "Driving While Black"; or worse, becoming target practice for "law enforcement," like West African immigrant Amadou Diallo, who, while standing, unarmed, in the lobby of his apartment building in New York City, was shot forty-one times by police officers who had taken the oath to "protect and serve."

This night, I thought about the decades and centuries that had passed without apologies. Marianne was saying, "I acknowledge to you the evils that have occurred here, in your life and in the lives of your ancestors." And I was thinking that no one had ever offered that to my parents—to my mother growing up in segregated Selma, Alabama, to my father who had to leave Kansas to find more tolerance and respect in the Pacific Northwest. My mind recalled no stories passed down through the generations of apologies to my grandparents or their grandparents, none to our enslaved ancestors, to Africa for its centuries-long rape and subsequent colonialism. The weight of all this made me begin to weep right there in that church. The experience of atonement was new for me, and I couldn't stop the flood of emotion that accompanied this new experience. First I chastised myself for not being able to stop the tears from welling up in my eyes, blurring my view of Marianne in the far front of the room as well as the women beside me whose hands I held. *Don't you cry. Don't you dare cry in front of these people.* But the tears came anyway as I heard the words I never expected—or even allowed myself to hope—to hear from *one* white person in my lifetime, much less the hundreds gathered on this night.

"God bless your children unto all generations . . ." I heard them say, and I thought of my daughter, whom I had recently taken to Ghana to see the slave castle at Elmina and its notorious "Door of No Return." I bowed my head, and silently gave in to my emotion.

Hugs were exchanged and the lecture ended. After wiping my face and gathering my composure, I waited in a long line to thank Marianne Williamson for her courage, her boldness to speak the taboo, to have a real conversation about race, to have the nerve and the sincerity to pray for atonement. My words felt inadequate. Hers, however, had been healing. Marianne was in touch with her ultimacy.

💚 *Your Ultimacy Journal** 💚

What does ultimacy mean to you? What changes do you need to make to become your "ultimate," best self?

In what ways are you:

- *Unique*

- *Unusual*

- *Unequaled*

- *Unbought and unbossed*

- *Ultracool*

What do you think our country and our world needs in order to have a spiritual uprising?

*If you don't want to write in this book, make a copy of this page, or take out the notebook, blank book, laptop, PC, or PDA you use for your journal to answer these questions.

RELAXATION

Relax! It's a one-word command that sounds so simple. *Relax, forget about it!* That's just what we need to do much more often than we actually do. The reality is that too many of us have a more intimate relationship with stress—the opposite of relaxation. Some of us can tell you all about the things that stress us out: job pressures, financial straits, relationship complexities, parenting responsibilities. But few of us can quickly rattle off the antidotes to stress; the tried-and-true ways we de-stress, rejuvenate, get refreshed and revived.

This third soulful secret for finding your purpose and minding your mission is relaxation, because most of us put the needs of others before our own, which in effect means we put ourselves last. When we leave our own needs for last—or worse, never get to them at all—we can become resentful, evil, hostile, maybe even abusive. Who needs that? If we take care of ourselves, we'll have more health, patience, love, happiness, and joy to share with others. That's not selfish—it's self-care.

Just like a mother-to-be who has to take care of herself in order to take care of her unborn child, we need to nurture ourselves, eat healthfully, stop smoking and drinking, and put our feet up every once in a while. Only by doing that can we give our loved ones our best. Before a baby is born, a mother's concern for the child's health is expressed by her attention to her own health. Before you can be a good caretaker to your children, a help to your elders, and a success at your job, you have to take care of yourself first. Sometimes that ultimate caring and concern may even mean bed rest. Don't wait for a doctor's orders to get yours.

After all, while you're taking care of others, who is taking care of you? You deserve and need nurturing just as much as the people you are caring for. So remember what my mother always says: "No one can take better care of you than *you*."

It's like filling up a car with gas before a journey. How can a car make the trip unless it has the fuel it needs, unless it's tuned up and in good condition? Tune up your body (exercise), give it the premium fuel (healthy food), and get regular checkups to be sure you're in optimum condition. That's the mind-set we need to be our best—for our families, our community, and to reach our own goals.

Whether the success you desire is of the fast-lane, climb-the-corporate-ladder type or the joy of inner peace that balance in your life provides, or both, and everything in between, it all starts with taking care of self.

Of course, what's easy to say is often hard to do. Self-care often seems like a luxury when you are stressed out. Family dysfunction, sudden illness, job layoffs, financial problems, relationship strain, and other troubles we can't seem to control enter our lives and throw us into crisis. And often, dealing with those crises becomes part of our lifestyle. Stress becomes just another modus operandi of our lives. When that happens, it becomes all the more important to react—not with emotion, but by taking control of your attitude and your actions.

Let's see how well you do that now. Here's a little quiz (don't stress it—it's easy):

Are You Controlling Stress or Is Stress Controlling You?

Respond to the following questions or statements.

1. Most of the time, I feel more blessed than stressed.

    A. You got that right

    B. I don't *think* so

    C. Who are you talking to? Not me

2. I exercise

    A. Every day

    B. Sometimes

    C. What do you call exercise?

3. I eat

    A. Mainly junk and fast food—I'm busy!

    B. Nutritiously most of the time, but sometimes I eat "whatever" on the run

    C. Like I wrote a book called *Good and Healthy*

4. At work, when difficult people get on my last nerve

    A. I let them—and anyone else within the sound of my voice—have it!

    B. I pray

    C. I wait, calm down, then try to resolve the problem

5. My love relationship is

    A. Nonexistent

    B. On the rocks

    C. Hot

6. If given my pick of jobs, I would choose

    A. A challenging, high-powered position—if I pull it off it could mean big money and prestige

    B. A job that's suited to my talents and skills

    C. One that allows me the most time with my family—I need a life!

7. I "do unto others"

    A. All the time

    B. Only to those who do unto me

    C. When possible—I take care of others, but I also take care of myself

8. When was the last time I took a vacation?

    A. A what?

    B. Sometime last year

    C. I'm on one now!

9. My sleeping habits are best described as follows:

    A. I'm late to bed, early to rise; too many things going on and problems on my mind

    B. I'm what you'd call an average sleeper

    C. Can't get enough of it: I'm a deep sleeper, hard to awaken

10. I have the following number of children under age twelve?

    A. Three or more

    B. One or two

    C. None

11. My method of disciplining children is

    A. To yell at the little hard-heads—they could run into traffic!

    B. To negotiate with them; treat them like adults and they'll act like them

    C. To use eye contact, speaking firmly

12. In the last year, how many days have I stayed home from work?

    A. I'm home now on disability

    B. A few; less than the company allows

    C. Never, my job makes me feel good!

13. In the last year, I have been hospitalized (except for childbirth)

    A. Twice or more

    B. Once

    C. None

14. I keep my house and my space at work

    A. A mess. I'm organizationally challenged

    B. Neat enough to not embarrass me if someone drops by

    C. I'm a neat freak and proud of it!

15. I usually stay mad at someone

    A. Forever

    B. Just long enough to take revenge

    C. Not long; I don't hold a grudge

16. If I were at an airport waiting to go on a long-awaited vacation, and the flight were delayed over an hour, I would

A. Cuss out the gate agent and threaten never to fly that airline again

B. Complain to people sitting around me

C. Do nothing—it wouldn't help anyway

17. What's my social style?

A. I am highly selective, so I can't be out with just anybody

B. You could call me "socially active"

C. I mainly party for good causes, like fundraisers

18. People borrow money from me

A. All the time, and never pay me back

B. Sometimes, but I set up a repayment plan

C. I believe in "Neither a lender nor a borrower be"

19. Safe sex is

A. More trouble than it's worth

B. Free entertainment!

C. A stress buster

20. My outlook on life is

A. What goes around, comes around

B. Life is what you make it

C. Don't worry, be happy

Scoring: Just so you wouldn't be too stressed out while taking this test, I thought I'd make it easy for you. And as you could probably tell, this quiz is not scientific. With the exception of the first two questions— which had the "stressed out" answer (usually A) and the "under control" answer (C) switched—I tried to make it pretty obvious that if you answered mostly Cs, that means you are handling stress very well. If your answers were mainly Bs, you handle stress moderately. If you are an A lady, let me give you a hug right now—you need some tender loving care! Keep reading for some strategies on how to tame the tension. One common stress buster is humor, and I hope you found the quiz to provide just that.

Let's back up and think about just what stress *is*. I would say it's the accumulation of daily assaults on our minds and emotions, and our reactions to the complications or our frustrations in handling them. I like to separate stress "assaults" as follows:

Baby taps: Little hits, like the kind a rambunctious toddler might give you. What I mean is:

- Waiting a long time for a bus when you're late

- Having words with someone who cuts in front of you in a line

- Answering the phone just as someone hangs up

Spankings: Remember when you'd get a spanking and then tell everybody, "It didn't even hurt!"? In the stress category, those are assaults that hit us hard, but from which we usually rebound. For example:

- When a bill collector sends us a dunning notice

- When we have performance anxiety (taking an exam, starting a new job)

- Having a heated argument with a lover

Knockouts: These are the bouts that take you out for the count!

- Abusive relationships

- Caring for an ill relative (or being in ill health yourself)

- Divorce

In fact, that last category could also be called "bad stress." *Heart & Soul* reported on a Duke University Medical Center study of African American women that identified their ten most common stressors:

1. Loss of loved ones through death, divorce, relocation, drug addiction, or incarceration

2. Strained male-female relationships

3. Concern for children's well-being

4. Caretaking responsibilities

5. Erosion of social values and the impact on our families and community

6. Job pressure

7. Job discrimination

8. Social stereotypes

9. Intraracial barriers (as a result of differences in socioeconomic level, education, and skin color)

10. Financial burdens

Okay, okay, so you already know what causes you great stress. If you're like most women, you live with stress and you have no problem identifying it. But did you know that there is such a thing as *good* stress? That's right. Good stress is when you get stressed out about something that will eventually give you pleasure. Such as:

- Planning a wedding

- Having a baby

- Getting a promotion at work

- Moving to a new home

That's the good stuff that may make you crazy now, but one day it will be recalled with joy and laughter. Recognizing and separating "good stress" from "bad stress" can make all the difference in your outlook on and management of stress.

Whether you're dealing with the good, the bad, or the ugly, here are some ways to calm down:

🍃 20 *Tension Tamers* 🍃

1. Pray

2. Meditate

3. Read a religious or spiritual book

4. Get a massage

5. Play your favorite CD

6. Drink chamomile tea

7. Take a candlelit bubble bath

8. Write in a journal

9. Exercise

10. Take "an armchair vacation" by flipping through travel brochures or visiting resort Web sites

11. Take a nap

12. Let your imagination run wild

13. Call a close friend

14. Revert to infantile behavior with your mama

15. Try yoga or tai chi

16. Take a walk

17. Read a good book

18. Laugh

19. Have sensual, consensual, protected sex with someone you love

20. Forget about whatever's bothering you!

The day after I wrote the previous list, I had "one of those days," the kind that "makes you wanna holler, throw up both your hands." The source of my stress was a bunch of stuff, including feelings of being overwhelmed by the tasks at hand and PMS—which at my age stands not only for Premenstrual Syndrome, but also what I call Premenopausal Silliness. So, I thought it was a good time to put the stress-reduction list to the test. I chose Tension Tamer #5: Play your favorite CD.

Sitting at my desk, where I was working on no less than four frustrating projects at once, I decided that instead of pulling out my nappy hair, I would turn on my tape player. My strategy is to keep a favorite CD in the player, a tape in the box, and the radio on the smooth jazz station—all in case of emergencies such as this. Frantic and full of anxiety, like a junkie desperate for a fix, I pushed the "Play" button on my CD player.

The disk began to spin. The opening bars of the song, mainly percussion, established the beat. The lines of the frown I didn't even know I had, began to ease. My head started bobbing. The arms and shoulders got to going up and down in rhythm. My fingers began to snap. Next thing I knew I was up on my feet. Mouth just going, singing along. Body dancing like I was at some jammin' party. By the time the cut was over, my previous frown had been replaced by a longer-lasting smile. I hadn't left the room, yet I was in a different place than I had been just five minutes before.

Then, I decided that since I was up and moving, I might as well go out for a walk. I changed into my workout clothes and sneaks, and headed for the park. Ninety minutes later, I was back at my computer, refreshed, less anxious, thinking more clearly, dealing with it all. The stress list had saved me! That's why I am confident it can work for you, too. (You may want to write the list on a piece of paper and carry it with you in your pocketbook in case of a stress emergency.)

Knowing what is effective (as well as healthy) for you is the key—

it's your own soulful secret. Although any one thing may not work at every stressful time, if you arm yourself with an arsenal of stress strategies, you'll be better prepared to choose your weapon of self-defense. I find that I don't always need to (nor can I find the time to) get up and leave a stressful situation. There are times when I'm trying to sort through a dilemma, and I find that doing something as mundane as cleaning the kitchen helps my mental state. Sound nuts? I think it works like this: taking the clean dishes out of the dishwasher, putting them in their place, stacking and organizing the cups, plates, pots and pans, and loading the dirty dishes, gives me a feeling of accomplishment. If I can clean up the mess in the kitchen, I can clean up the mess in my mind. While I'm cleaning the kitchen, I often think of solutions for the other mess. And all this from a person who used to get in big trouble as a kid for shirking my dish-washing duties! Who would have thought that this formerly stressful chore would one day become a stress *reliever?* The Lord *does* work in mysterious ways!

Another stress-prevention strategy might be a private pursuit or a personal passion. For example, very few people know that throughout my childhood, I studied classical piano at a conservatory. I was no child prodigy, but the twelve years of lessons every Monday at four-thirty, gave me a precious gift. It didn't give me a career in music (although my first job at fourteen was playing piano for the church choir), or even a desire to play for my friends. Yet, in my moments of solitude, of melancholy, of relaxation, I often sit down at my piano and listen to my own renditions of Beethoven, Mozart, Bach, and Debussy. Or I open my hymn book and play songs I have known all my life—hymns that my grandmother knew, that my daughter has heard in church, that my father hummed around the house, that my mother still sings in the choir. And I soothe myself.

Sometimes just mentally stepping out of the anxiety through prayer, meditation, or reflection can bring an instant oasis of calm. Within this peace, you can find the inner strength to find solutions to your challenges.

♥ *Adventures in Bed* ♥

There's on-the-spot stress busting, and then there's prevention. Most people do have a favorite way to stave off stress. Mine is called "having an adventure in bed."

Whenever I mention such an adventure, I love seeing the way people react. "Oh, what was that again?" they ask with their ears perked up, as though they had been sleeping through everything I'd said up until then. "Did you say 'adventure in bed'? What's *that?*" they ask with a sly look on their face. I am rarely disappointed by how merely saying the word "bed" gets folks' attention and has them convinced you're talking sex.

But my adventure in bed isn't about sex. Though it *could* be. What I'm talking about is hibernating in bed one morning a week—or how about at least once a month? It's my interpretation of the biblical day of rest. *On the seventh day He rested.* I figure you can't get a better goal model than that!

On the day you decide to stay in bed, you can do whatever you want to do—even if that means doing nothing at all. For me, hanging out in bed is the closest thing I have to returning to the womb. It pretty much ensures that I won't have to deal with any stress that day. It calms me. It's stress prevention at its best.

Family traditions come in all kinds of quirky rituals. This one was passed down from my mother. One of my earliest remembrances is of Saturday mornings when, as a baby, I would get up early and toddle into my parents' bedroom. My father, an attorney, usually had office hours on Saturdays, so my mother, whose work as a schoolteacher meant keeping up with thirty energetic second-graders (and then dealing with her own three kiddies at home), would be alone in bed sleeping late. Not about to let me or anyone else disturb her rest before she was ready, Mom would say to me, "Come here, Sweetie. Come get into bed with Mommy." Then I'd curl up with her in her bed, and the next thing I'd know, I'd be back asleep.

It wasn't always easy to chill on weekends several years later when I was old enough for Saturday morning choir rehearsal. My mother's own tune had changed; she considered our church's junior choir rehearsal more important than hanging out in bed. By the time I was seventeen, I had a job at a clothing store, having to arrive before the store opened on the weekends. At college, I was back in the swing of lounging in the dorm until *whenever* (but up and dressed in time to eat in the med school cafeteria, where scoping out handsome docs-in training was about as much sport as my roommates and I could muster). After college, as a young single sister in the big city, I used the Saturday respite from work to take a long bath, wash my hair, give myself a facial, and otherwise pamper myself using my bed as my base of operation. Not exactly an adventure *in* bed, but *on* it. Same principle.

When I had my own baby, I did as my mother had done. I didn't encourage my own little sweetie, Anique, to think that 6 A.M. was an appropriate time to wake everybody else in the house up—especially on Saturdays. When she was a baby, I would breast-feed her, then take her back to bed with me. She would play around with her toes or a toy, but after a while—you guessed it—she'd go back to sleep. At the very least she would allow me some more shut-eye. Soon she started staying in her own bed or playing quietly in her room.

But then, my daughter got old enough to take ballet lessons on Saturdays. Of course, the classes for the tiny tots are always at 8 or 9 A.M.—just like another day of going to work. And I thought taking her there was my job. Don't *mommies* take daughters to ballet? I thought about switching my day of rest to Sundays, but unless one is watching a church service on television or listening to a church radio broadcast, it's not easy to lie around and attend church, too. In trying to do it all, I sacrificed all my private time. It made me happy to see my daughter's talent emerging on Saturdays, and on Sundays I was spiritually uplifted after church, but I was cranky and evil a lot of the rest of the time.

Fortunately, my husband (whose high-energy level seems to go on "automatic pilot" until the Sunday afternoon football games, when he takes a time-out) volunteered for Saturday ballet-class shift, and I was able to regain my "bed time."

I'm not alone in my desire to get more rest. Lots of people in this country my age are trying to stave off burnout the very same way. I once saw a television magazine show that stated that baby boomers with demanding jobs often incur a phenomenon called sleep debt. People are so hyped up during the week—working hard, staying up late helping with homework, doing household chores, or trying to have a social life—that on weekends they attempt to erase their sleep debt by getting up late or by taking naps. The promise that technology would give us more leisure time has backfired. Instead, it has allowed women and men to work more—and consequently be more stressed out.

Some folks just aren't having it, though. They're heading stress off at the pass. Author J. California Cooper is one of them. "I live in the bed," she once told me without shame in an interview I conducted for *Essence*. "My wardrobe is nightgowns. I don't see any sense in getting dressed if you're at home. I write my books in longhand in bed, and when I finish the stories I go to my computer a few steps away. That's because in the bed is where I'm most relaxed. When you relax, your brain is the only thing you have to work. It doesn't mean you're lazy."

Not only working at home, but working at home in bed may be a burgeoning trend—and not just relegated to weekends. I was reading *Working Woman* magazine's cover story on "The Top 500 Women-Owned Businesses" of 1999 when the photo of the woman who owned the company ranked #315 caught my attention. Kristen Schaffner-Irvin, owner of Team Petroleum in Huntington Beach, California, was pictured in a "power pose" in her work environment—stretched out in pajamas across her bed with cell phone in hand, laptop on the comforter, and a smile on her face. Schaffner-Irvin started her $34 million business so that she could be home with her children. "My competitors used to joke that I took my laptop to bed with me," she is quoted as saying. And they weren't too far from wrong.

Maybe more people would understand why I like to hang out in bed (and would even try it themselves) if they knew that staying in bed can make you rich. One day when I was lying in my bed, I picked up a book my husband had left around called *Money Is My Friend* by Phil Laut. "This book is about achieving FINANCIAL FREEDOM," the book yelled in capital letters. "Building a PROSPERITY CONSCIOUS-NESS is the way to ensure your financial success."

I dipped inside this book, and couldn't believe my eyes. Much to my surprise, along with several other suggestions for improving your self-esteem as a means of ultimately increasing your financial success (the message being care for yourself and you'll be able to perform better), I found a message that really hit home: *Stay in bed all day once per week* (emphasis mine).

Discussing my bedbug habits with an early riser, I realized that she was having a hard time grasping the concept. In her attempt to understand, she said, "Oh, I get it; you take to your bed." Not quite. I don't do it as a reaction to illness or to anything depressing, but just to renew myself. To keep sane. To recharge myself by turning my mind off and claiming peace and solitude. It's like going to a beach and sunbathing. But instead of spreading out my blanket on the sand, I spread it out on my bed. My time in the sack is chill-out time to do whatever I want—or to do nothing. And for me, that's a stress-free, self-care adventure.

Trying to carve out an adventure in bed when you're a mother takes some maneuvering. Here are some strategies:

- Carpool, so you can trade off chauffeuring duties

- Gang errands for later in the day

- Find open-late services, such as a cleaners that you can go to after work instead of on Saturday

- Ditto for grocery shopping

- Go to a hairstylist and manicurist who have Sunday hours (or do the touch-ups yourself at home)

- Ditto the manicurist (or do it yourself at home)

- Trade off baby-sitting with a friend or relative who has children the same age as yours

- Enlist the help of a teenager (a niece, a nephew, or a young neighbor) to keep your child occupied or who can drive the child to weekend sports practices, birthday parties, and the like

- If you are divorced, revel in the weekends your children spend with their father. If you're married, have your spouse take the kids off your hands anyway. Schedule a "Day with Daddy" adventure for Saturdays or Sundays.

❧ *Time-Out* ❧

You've heard the joke: A kid is asked, "What's your favorite period at school?" And he answers, "Recess."

Well, that's me. My very favorite activity is comparable: Vacation. I try hard to be either on vacation or planning one. Sometimes, I'm on vacation *and* planning the next one. I love to travel, so I'm always thinking of where in the world I want to go. I want to see as much of the planet as I can before I leave it. It's my belief that God put us in the world in one spot, then gave us legs, cars, trains, buses, boats, and planes in order to move around to enjoy the rest of His creation. Vacation, whether you stay at home or travel, is refreshing.

Now, this country really doesn't give their employees enough vacation. Most people have about two weeks out of the year to spend away from their jobs. In other countries, particularly European countries, six weeks is the norm. I remember seeing a guy on television say that he wanted to run for President of the United States on the platform of what he called the Six-Week Initiative—the premise that all Americans should have the right to six weeks of vacation. If I could have only remembered the name of that man, I just might have given him my vote as a write-in candidate!

I've worked with people who never use all their vacation days. Some have been on the same job for enough years to have accumulated, say, four months of vacation, and they just can't break away from the job. They feel no one else can do their job but them, that they are so busy they can't carve out time for a break. But those people are usually the same ones who are the most stressed out. They're the ones who use the word "burnout" most often. They also often have the messiest offices because they can't clear out their schedule and they can't clear out their work space. They can't organize their office or their time out of it. These are the people who need time out the most.

Of course, many of us want time off and would be more than happy to take it because we can't stand our jobs or our bosses or the people we work with—but we just don't have as much time off as we would like. Here are some alternative ways to grab your own mental breaks.

TIME-OUT FOR A SECOND

- Picture yourself doing what you like to do on vacation
- Think of a loved one
- Say an affirmation

TIME-OUT FOR A MINUTE

- Take six deep breaths to the count of ten
- Sing your favorite song
- Get up and walk around the room

TIME-OUT FOR AN HOUR

- Browse in your favorite bookstore
- Take an exercise class
- Send an e-mail to your honey or visit your favorite Web site

TIME-OUT FOR ONE DAY

- Spend the day with your favorite person
- Pursue a new sport
- Take a day trip

TIME-OUT FOR A WEEKEND

- Find a spiritual retreat
- Get lost on a drive in the country and make impromptu reservations at the closest inn or bed and breakfast
- Visit a friend you haven't seen in years

TIME-OUT FOR A WEEK OR LONGER

If you've got a week off, I probably don't have to tell you what to do with it. More than likely, you've been anticipating the vacation time to do things you usually don't have time for. If you're one of the wonderful people in the teaching profession with the good fortune to have summers off, you know that time taken to travel, spend time with family, make extra money at a summer job, or in classes that upgrade or refresh your skills, goes by oh so quickly. So it's still a good idea to plan a week or so just to do things that *you* want to do, rather than those that are expected of you. If you use your entire summer vacation baby-sitting your grandchildren, or even globetrotting in Africa, plan time to do *nothing* before resuming your regular work schedule.

TIME-OUT FOR A MONTH OR TWO

Too few of us get this kind of time-out. So what we don't get, we sometimes need to take.

Most of us think of teachers and college professors and say, "If only I could be that lucky." Well, I did that at one point myself. I thought, *If only I could have a summer off from work, I could regroup and not feel so burnt out all the time.* I wanted to see what it would be like to go off to Europe for the summer, like folks you read about in books and magazines. The feeling just wouldn't leave me, and after one four-day trip to Paris around the time of my fortieth birthday, I became determined to make it happen.

Unlike in the academic world, there was no such thing as a sabbatical where I worked in corporate America—and magazines are corporations. I decided that since I wanted a sabbatical, and there was no company policy that would grant me one, I would try to invent one. My motto has always been "nothing ventured, nothing gained." If I never asked my boss for a sabbatical, I would never get one. And if I asked and she said no, then I still wouldn't get one, but at least I would have had the satisfaction of knowing I had asked. And if I asked and she said yes, then—bingo! Well, the latter is just what happened. After fifteen years at *Essence,* I loved my job, but I was tired—plain and simple. And I wanted to try my hand at writing a novel. I would write when I could grab a few hours here and there, but working full-time, while raising one child full-time and three more (stepchildren) part-time, left little time for pursuing my dream. So, I made up my mind to take the vacation of a lifetime. Here's how I pulled it off—and how you can, too:

First, figure out how to pay for it. During my business trip to Paris in February, I had no idea how I would pay for a nonbusiness trip in July. I didn't have much money in the bank either. But what I had was the ability to obsess about what I wanted! I thought and thought and thought about every little detail. I made lists:

- My paycheck—How would I be able to afford to go anywhere, much less pay the mortgage, if I had to take the time off without pay? I decided to save all my vacation time to cover one month, then use my sick time for more days, and take off the rest without pay. Fortunately, there were some expenses I wouldn't have by not going to work—commuting fare, lunch money, and daycare for the baby (more on that later).

- The airfare—I decided to use my frequent flyer miles so I wouldn't have to pay. However, if I hadn't had that option, I would have looked for a deal. If travel is in your plans, you may be able to find "summer sales" on vacation packages. Or plan your travel in the "low season" of your destination, when fares are at their most affordable. Research travel deals on the Internet.

- The hotel—I studied travel guides and found a low-cost American-owned hotel in Paris, then I called and bargained (in English, since it was an American hotel) for a lower rate for staying more than ten

.days. In addition, I decided to contact a childhood friend who lived in another part of the country to ask if I could stay with her for one week of my four in France. She said yes (whew!).

Stay with friends, renew old ties, freeload as long as you can stand it and they can stand you (but avoid wearing out your welcome by agreeing on the length of stay before you arrive), or check into less luxurious digs than you normally would (I once traveled in Central America staying in hostels, which at age twenty-two was a great ten-dollar adventure).

- Travel money—I decided to save $1,500 for travel expenses. That meant depositing a certain amount more in my savings account religiously on each payday. No new clothes, no dinners out, no movies. Deprivation for later reward. I budgeted, dug out an underused credit card and charged the hotel expense, and paid cash for everything else. As fate would have it, I was so frugal with my cash on the trip (taking advantage of the freebie Continental breakfast and then only having dinner—sometimes at a Paris Mickey D's) that I could have paid for most of the hotel with the leftover cash.

If you are in the habit of saving money, it won't be hard to squeeze more juice from the onion of your paycheck. But if you are in credit-card debt or otherwise in over your head financially, it may be best to make digging out from under your first step toward taking time out. Perhaps the thought of a time-out will serve as a motivating force to clean up your debts and start saving.

OTHER WAYS TO TAKE TIME OFF

- Get a grant for a research project or a scholarship to study abroad

- Find an internship

- Get a second job and save money for your trip

Examine your job benefits. Let's face it, if you've been on your job only a year or two, it's not likely you'll be granted an extended leave. And it would be pretty nervy to even ask. But if you have an occupation that affords that type of absence, or if you have an employer who is open to unpaid time off, you could ask for a leave of, maybe, a month (some companies give you four weeks vacation after five years anyway). Or you could ask for two months if you've been a faithful staffer for ten years. You've got to have some loyalty stored up to use as a negotiating chip before you go trippin' (and of course I mean that in the nicest way).

Next, decide what to call your time-out. I decided that I needed a "sabbatical"—a concept that wouldn't sound like I just wanted to goof off, but that sounded sophisticated and worthwhile. Even telling people I planned to write a book was more information than I was ready to share. It wasn't like I was some big-time novelist or something. I was just following my fantasy. So the more vague "sabbatical" worked. Other suggestions: leave of absence, extended leave, bonus time off.

Figure out the best time to leave. It's a good idea to give some thought to when the slowest periods on your job might be, when you would be missed the least. Would it be when most people are going on vacation anyway, or when there's a full shop of employees to cover your duties? Then try to match that with your personal needs. For example, I needed to take the time off when my daughter would be on summer break and spending her vacation with my parents. Like many African American mothers in the North who used to send kids "down South" in the summer, I had a fortunate—blessed!—arrangement with my mother for Anique to spend summers "out West" with her in Seattle. This was the time I could escape, which also happened to be the best time workwise.

Make sure you're covered. If you may need to take a leave, do you know who would do your job? Will that person be able to carry out your responsibilities while you take a personal time-out? If you decide to take a leave without pay, is there a freelancer who can come in full-time? Is there a temp the company can hire using the money they won't be paying you? Can you work overtime to do your job in advance? Think as you suspect your boss will; by anticipating any objections, you can come up with a solution before you approach her.

Draw up a plan. Make your request in writing. Write a memo or proposal outlining your request and how you suggest your job get done without you. Then make an appointment to present your plan, after which you should allow a week or more for a response.

Be ready to follow through. You know the saying, "Be careful what you ask for, because you just might get it"? Well, ya never know! If your request is denied, be sure you understand the reason, so you can plan to try it again with a better strategy. But if your request is granted, as mine was in 1992 by my fabulous boss at the time, Susan L. Taylor, then be ready to follow your dream.

By the way, I did take that sabbatical and I did write 220 pages of my novel while happily holed up in a cheap Paris hotel and later at my friend Olivia's lovely Lyon apartment. But the book was never published. I may not be the person to write the Great American Novel, but at least I learned that about myself while on a much-needed time-out. It was self-care in the first degree. If I, who thought I'd never have another summer vacation off after graduating from college, could do it, so can you.

Simplifying and Signifying

Sometimes, the yearning for time-out can turn into an opportunity to change your life. My own brother, André Wooten, had had it up to *here* with the stress of being a prosecuting attorney in Seattle. So he decided to use the money from the sale of an old house he had lived in and lovingly renovated to take a year off and see what it would be like to live in Hawaii. André had been a champion swimmer as a child, and he soon realized that in Hawaii, he could practice law *and* go surfing after work. He decided to take the bar examination for the State of Hawaii. I'm happy to report that André has had a successful law practice in Honolulu for almost twenty years.

He even found a soulmate to marry! Daphne Barbee of Milwaukee had the same idea—being an attorney in a warm-weather climate. Together, André and Daphne have made a lifestyle out of their common soulful secret—relaxation in a sunny paradise. If you should visit

Hawaii, you just may see them—a tall, dreadlocked brother at the beach pulling a surfboard out of his van just before dusk, and an athletic-bodied sister taking hula lessons on the sand. If you run into them, give them the Hawaiian soul greeting—a fist with the thumb and pinkie up.

💟 Worn Out at Work 💟

A woman calling herself "Trapped by Success" complained to Ann Landers that spending eight to ten hours a day in the office never leaves enough time for her children. Going to meetings, taking business trips, having business breakfasts, lunches, and sometimes business dinners, and using her vacation days for family emergencies has left her with little leisure time ("I haven't read a book for fun in five years"). "Is there a way out?" she asked. Landers advised her that there was, but that it meant giving up something—a salary increase, a promotion, or maybe the job itself. Women must ask themselves if the price of success is worth the personal sacrifices.

Unfortunately, it's not just the price of success many of us have to weigh—it's the price of providing for our children the kinds of opportunities we feel we want them to have. For example, if you feel that your child would perform better academically in private school, your salary may be necessary to pay for it. And if you are a single parent, the weight of the family's expenses for these things lies solely on you.

So if you're worn out at work, there are some choices you can make, based on your situation. Review your options, think hard about a sure-win plan, and act on it. Here are a few ideas to consider:

- *Change your job.* Like the college administrator, it is possible to get a higher-paying job doing the same work for another employer. Research the competition. Who has the reputation for treating employees well? Are any companies known for providing generous family benefits?

- *Work part-time.* Some jobs offer more flexibility than others. For example, according to the U. S. Department of Labor, the fifth leading occupation of African American women in 1996 was retail sales worker. Its report on "Black Women in the Labor Force" states that although many salesclerks and other service occupations do not offer high wages and often come without health care and other fringe benefits, they frequently "offer flexibility in work hours not generally characteristic in many other occupational groups." An employee may be able to decide if she prefers to work part-time (helpful for students and mothers of young children) or full-time (if you are trying to climb the store's management ladder). Some women are creating part-time jobs at companies that haven't traditionally had them. I have a neighbor who works at a magazine and is the mother of two small boys. A copy editor, she has negotiated a three-day workweek.

- *Job share.* Another woman I know, who has no children, works at a magazine three days a week and runs a real estate business on the other days, including weekends, when she shows properties to prospective homeowners. In her case, her boss decided to split her job in half, and have someone else come in the second part of the week.

- *Work at home.* A sister-friend of mine called me and said that she had decided that she wanted to work at home. She's an investment banker, and that's not a profession that one would normally think of as a home-based business, but she'll probably pull it off because there's a growing trend of people who are tired of spending so much of their lives in the workplace. And many of them are doing something about it. Many companies are allowing their employees more flexibility. People with tech-intensive jobs are good candidates for working at home. If you are in a field in which much of your time is spent working on the computer (if you are a Web site designer or content provider), you may be expected to work at home.

🖤 *Enlightened Employers* 🖤

Increasingly, employers are responding to the stress calls of their workers. And some more enlightened managers are telling their workaholics to get a life. With employee burnout contributing to decreased productivity as a result of low morale, high turnover, and more absenteeism, companies are making efforts to help workers alter their work schedules. Here are some of the ways employers are trying to alleviate the problem:

- *A company picnic.* A long-standing policy of many corporations is the summer company picnic. Depending on how large the company is, these events can be as small as a barbecue or as large as a carnival. They give employees time with their family, social interaction with colleagues, and a day away from the office.

- *After-work sports.* Another tradition at companies, usually those with a large number of male employees. The good ol' summer softball games help you cream the competition in a healthy way (and work off some stress, too).

- *Family leave days.* With many workers having children later and their parents living longer, they find themselves in the "sandwich generation," squished between caring for children under eighteen and watching out for elders. When elder parents can no longer take care of themselves, middle-aged workers often need to take time off to care for them, or to arrange for elder daycare, or to take a parent to the doctor. On the other hand, the same worker may have to pick up a sick child from the nurse's office at school in the middle of a busy day at the office. Compassionate employers understand this and allow for "family leave" days.

  In 1993, then President Clinton signed into law the Family and Medical Leave Act, which guarantees up to twelve weeks off without pay to care for a new child or needy family member. In February 2000, the President proposed a $20 million study to find new ways for the law to be expanded to include paid leave for employees of small companies who are not covered by the 1993 law. In his weekly radio address, President Clinton, recalling his mother's struggle as a single parent, said, "I've often wondered how my own mother, when she was a young widow, would have been able to go away to train as a nurse if my grandparents hadn't been there to take care of me. My mother and I were lucky. So were many other American families. But none of our families should have to rely on luck alone."

- *Stress-survival seminars.* PricewaterhouseCoopers has a two-day stress survival clinic, *USA Today* reports, where participants meet with a physician, nutritionist, and psychiatrist to focus on how to better cope with pressure.

- *Refer employees to psychological services.* Some stress can lead to depression, anxiety, or addictions, which companies that care about well-being attempt to stave off by giving referrals to 12-step programs, psychologists, or other therapy-based programs. Some have even begun to employ in-house therapists.

- *Pay fitness fees.* Today more companies have either on-premises fitness centers, arrangements with a gym, or give reimbursements for health-club membership. Some companies even set up space for massage therapists to give back rubs on certain days of the month.

- *Provide meditation rooms.* From closet-size prayer rooms to large architecturally designed showcases for meditation, employers are carving out spaces that help workers just cope. One such impressive structure was built by Rodale Press, in Emmaus, Pennsylvania. The company created a Pueblo Indian–style "kiva," or "meditation area," in the middle of the main floor of one of the company's newer office buildings. The two-story meditation room with a rotunda skylight, is open to employees any time of day.

🍂 Dropping Out 🍂

There are always going to be those people who just can't take the stress, no matter what the company does or doesn't do to make work bearable. And for some folks, it's not the company itself, or even the nature of the work, but those *other people* they have to work with that drive them nuts. Volumes have been written about getting along with difficult people. On the flip side, some folks just are not meant to work for other folks. There are people who are entrepreneurial to the bone and cannot work well with or for others. They are people who just march to the rhythm of their own congas, and can't seem to follow anyone else's beat.

Others attempt to flee the urban corporate scene for "the simple life." Magazines are full of charming stories of couples who left high-powered jobs for the allure of the country, where they do who-knows-what to make a living.

Although that may seem like a fantasy, there is a virtual reality: With more companies operating in lean and mean fashion, and constantly assessing their bottom lines, there are more employee opportunities for buy-outs and early retirements. When a company sells off one of its divisions or experiences a merger, an employee's circumstances may also change. When these unexpected changes happen, what are your options?

- *Jump to the competition.* A United Airlines employee in Los Angeles was offered a buy-out of the equivalent of one year's pay. She thought about taking the year off before starting another job, but when Continental Airlines offered her a job right away, she took it and saved the severance (after deducting a small amount for a much-needed vacation).

- *Change careers.* When my friend Karen's job as a business consultant in Washington, D.C., came to an end when her company was involved in a merger, she decided to take her severance pay and move back home to Montgomery. There, she studied interior design and finally followed her dream to open her own design firm. Someone else I know lived off her severance pay for a year while she contemplated her next move. She decided not to return to her high-stress corporate field, but to become a Web site editor, a job that allowed her to work from home.

- *Start a business.* Duh. That may seem like the most obvious option, but it always takes courage and serious planning to get a new venture off the ground. As most small businesses have only one or two employees—often just the owner—freelancing or becoming a consultant is another way to look at starting a business. (For more information on starting a business, take adult-education classes, research the tons of books for the how-tos, or contact the Small Business Administration.)

- *Go back to school.* It's never too late to learn something new. Older students are taking business classes, learning new skills, and obtaining more college degrees. Don't think you have the money for college? There's all kind of financial aid, not just for eighteen-year-olds fresh out of high school, but for anyone who needs it. A helpful book is *Money for College* by Erlene B. Wilson. The Internet also provides a wealth of information on financial aid. Some popular sites include:

  - *www.fastweb.com*

  - *www.finaid.com*

  - *www.scholaraid.com*

  - *www.scholarships.com*

💟 *Inspired Introspection* 💟

Sometimes you won't have the luxury of deciding to take "time out" or even "drop out" of the rat race for a while—instead a crisis arises and you're forced to improvise and deal with what life throws your way. When an overwhelming circumstance over which you have no control occurs, you may think that no degree of self-care or stress reduction can help. It's normal to sink into despair when devastating things happen to you. But many people are living examples of how we can all use misfortune to tap into our ultimate power and purpose. Maybe you know someone on whom you can model yourself. Or read a biography, or search for inspiring human-interest stories in newspapers, magazines, or on the Net, all of which can give you strength to confront your own challenges. If you reach deep inside yourself, you can turn tragedy into triumph.

❦ Relax, Refresh, Revive! ❦

A good old-fashioned weekend away with friends can do wonders to re-vive the spirit. The camaraderie of people who know you well, and whom you trust with your secrets, insecurities, hopes, and dreams can help to renew you and get you ready to face your challenges. I can tell you from personal experience that it works.

Two of my girlfriends and I are mad about spas. Since we all have birthdays that fall under the astrological sign of Capricorn, in the spirit of the movie *Same Time, Next Year,* we get together annually around our birthdays and celebrate by splurging on a hotel suite, pampering day-spa treatments, and an afternoon of shopping.

To plan a weekend of your own, I suggest you find a hotel that has a spa or stay in your favorite hotel and spa-hop to different places each day of the weekend. Over the years, we've also planned a weekend on the cheap and have saved money by spending the night at my house, and choosing just one day-spa and one treatment each. Another year we checked into a hotel suite, split the cost and went to one spa on Satur-day. In the future, we plan to go to a resort spa in the Caribbean. I know another group of women who meet at Rancho La Puerta Spa in Mexico for a weeklong program of pampering every single year! The choice is up to you and your budget, but do give it a try!

Whether you go away to re-create the benefits of precious self-indulgence, or can't wait and want to feel good right away, you can treat yourself to one of the tricks of the spa trade in the privacy of your own home with the following special pampering treatment.

How to Win the Rose Bowl

Create a rose petal milk foot bath in a bowl or a rose-covered warm-water body bath in your tub by following these instructions, from Doretha Levy, director of the Swissotel Park Avenue Spa:

1. Take the petals from a wilting bouquet of roses.

2. Put them in a large bowl filled with warm milk for a pedicure, or in a bathtub of warm water for a body bath. Let the petals sit a few minutes. The warm temperature will release the fragrant essential oils of the plant into the milk or water, and coat your pores as you bathe.

3. Afterward, collect the petals in a mesh shower cap or bag, and when the petals dry you will have a wonderful handmade sachet.

If you have simpler tastes, just draw yourself a nice hot bath, light a few candles, and take a long hot soak.

❧ *Your Relaxation Journal** ❧

Good stress I've had in my life:

The most frequent "bad stress" I experience:

My own favorite stress busters:

I would like to try:

    ——*An Adventure in Bed*

    ——*A Spa Weekend*

    ——*Time-out*

    ——*Inspired Introspection*

    ——*Other*———————————

. . . because the benefit would be:

I pledge to relax, refresh, and revive myself more often by (doing what?) . . .
(Decide what you'll do daily, weekly or monthly.)

*If you prefer not to write in this book, copy this page or take out your own journal to answer these questions.

POSITIVITY

You absolutely, positively *have* to stay positive. It's as simple as that and as difficult as that. Very few things of value are easy to achieve, so we have to maintain a positive attitude in order to stay focused. Positivity keeps us on the "up and up." It keeps us looking higher and moving forward, rather than looking down at how far we can fall. A positive attitude allows us to believe in ourselves, to hope, to expect, to achieve. Shaking off negativity and anger, we are more likely to be confident, to see humor in a challenging situation, and to act assertively. These are the qualities that can make change happen.

It is amazing to me that African Americans, who have lived through every wretchedness this country has to offer, can still manage to thrive. It's that positive mind-set that made Mahalia Jackson sing "Move on Up a Little Higher." Think of the positive affirmations of "We Shall Overcome" and "I Don't Feel Noways Tired." Then consider the difficult circumstances of the civil rights movement—that was a time when people really *did* feel overcome and *always* tired.

Such feats of the human spirit prove that all of us *can* be positive, even when the situation is negative. We can maintain optimism, even when the overwhelming odds point to pessimism. Now, I'm not saying it is *easy*, but I am saying it can be done, and that the struggles and triumphs of our ancestors are the proof.

On a trip to Ghana in 1999, my family and I visited the slave castles at Elmina. One of the enclaves we toured was the very castle in which the independent film *Sankofa* was filmed. The word *sankofa* means to "look back in order to move forward." In looking back at how those before us handled difficult situations, we can learn to handle our own—now and in the future. My observation is that through unspeakable horrors of the separation of family, the theft of culture and even language, the one thing no one could take was our foremothers' and forefathers' positive spirit of perseverance. And that spirit is always ours for the taking.

The Spirit of Perseverance

No matter who you are or what your background, when you move in a spirit of perseverance, you go forward resolutely (that is, with a fixed purpose) in spite of whatever difficulties may be in your way. You move ahead with persistence. You push away obstacles. In order to do any of these things, you have to stay positive.

But positivity doesn't necessarily mean being jolly all the time. It means being optimistic and hopeful in spite of the challenge. It means managing your emotions in an upbeat way. Here are some obstacles and emotions you may encounter along the path to your ultimate purpose:

Anger/Rage: The ineffective management of anger can have an adverse effect on your relationships, at work or at home. It can also affect your health, manifesting as headaches, stomach pain, feelings of distress, and high blood pressure. Uncontrolled rage can even affect your mental health.

What to do? Ronald B. Brown, Ph.D., president of Banks Brown in San Francisco, which specializes in diversity issues and rage management in the workplace, says rage doesn't have to be a bad thing. "It motivates you and fuels your drive. But how you harness it is what matters, so it doesn't take you down." He suggests that you first "acknowledge when you are having a rage response. Then evaluate the situation." For example, does your boss treat everyone abruptly, or just you? Try not to

take things personally. The problem may be the other person's
in your evaluation, you know you are to blame, do try to make
right immediately, rather than sink into self-doubt. Use your ene
positively.

Gossip: Do you find that there are certain people in your life who are
constantly spreading unkind rumors and talking about folks? They may
or may not be talking about you, but it is still a negative factor in your
life if someone is wasting your time with poisonous energy.

    What to do? There's a difference between talking about someone
maliciously and sharing news. I once discovered something that should
have been common sense, but I couldn't see it: If you don't want people talking negatively about you, don't talk negatively about other people. Sounds so simple, but it's so true. If you refuse to talk maliciously
about other people, then you will find that others will pick up your vibe.
I have found that malicious gossip tends to have a certain tone, an attitude. There's a difference between saying "Girl, did you hear that Miss
Thing got laid off today?" and "There were some layoffs at Boeing today
and, unfortunately, our friend was affected. Wonder what we can do
to help?"

Negaholics: These are the people whose M.O. is always "no." "No," you
shouldn't start your own business. "No," you don't need to buy a house if
you're single. "No," you shouldn't move to another city to marry that
man. "No," you don't need a college degree—you've already got a job,
don't you?

    Some people are addicted to being a negative influence and if you
look at their lives closely, you'll see that there's really not much going on.
You might look up to them because they're older than you, or make more
money than you, or they're your closest relative. But have the negaholics
in your life realized their own goals and dreams? Are they really the best
role models for the things you are trying to do? Why do we think our
closest friend knows how to advise us on everything?

    What to do? Surround yourself with people who have good vibes. If
you feel compelled to bounce all your ideas off someone close to you, at

n is open-minded and supportive. You don't
·st avoid people who get their jollies from

· field can provide good advice and support
chment, as can people in other areas of your life
iends. For example, about twenty years ago when I
st-feed my daughter, it was not a common thing to do.
iy women I talked to were unsupportive: "You won't know if
ting enough milk!" "What if she bites you?" But I found a sup-
. group, the La Leche League, that advised me by phone and gave
ne positive reinforcement—even in the middle of the night.

Worry: Obsessive worrying is another thing that can affect our well-being. Caution, carefulness, and concern are positive feelings that we
should have for ourselves and our loved ones. But constant worry over
imagined phenomena is destructive.

As a district-court judge, my late father often heard cases concerning freeway accidents. After so many pictures of horrible crashes and
untimely deaths, he himself began to fear driving on the freeway. That
was fine; we could understand his own reluctance, and we were patient
while he drove us to the airport by the back roads. But when he tried to
discourage everyone in the family from freeway driving, and would
badger us each time he knew we would be going someplace via a multi-
lane highway, we knew he was acting out of love, but thought he was being overly worried nonetheless.

What to do? Consider if the fears are really founded or not. In the
case of the freeway driving, for example, do most people on the freeway
get in accidents? No. But in my father's case, most of the car accidents
he adjudicated happened on the freeway, so that statistic threw the reality out of proportion. People who worry obsessively would do well to
remember the Serenity Prayer: *God grant me the serenity to accept the*
things I cannot change; Courage to change the things I can; And wisdom to
know the difference.

If you are the worrier, turn your concerns into positive action. • **Take**
a hike. Getting away from the source of your worry by exercising, can
occupy your mind and give you a different perspective—all while help-

ing you attain a healthier heart rate. • **Advocate.** Use that energy constructively to help others. My father's concern for our safety turned into public concern for highway safety.

I once gave Daddy a book that may help you: *Meditations for People Who (May) Worry Too Much* edited by Anne Wilson Schaef and Cheryl Woodruff.

💗 The Power of the Positive 💗

Turning negative forces into positive energies can give you the ability to do your work effectively, win promotions, and get raises. In addition, the wholesome management of your own counteractive feelings can be a positive force for your family and community. Here are some of the elements of positivity that can put you on the path to your purpose.

POSITIVE THINKING

Not everybody can blame the negaholics in their lives for holding them back. Some folks do that quite nicely on their own, thank you. Heeding a voice of habit that says "You can't do that," many people talk themselves into "making do." They convince themselves that they should "leave well enough alone." Since few outside forces have encouraged their ambitions or goals, they don't feel validated enough to make an effort. "Why bother?," the negative thinking goes.

Negative thinking, often borne of low self-esteem or lack of confidence, gives us negative results. Only with inner resolve can we change the "tape" in our heads to say "Yes, I can do it!"

"Yes" is the first key to positive thinking. Say it softly, and it sounds like a prayer. Say it loudly, and it practically propels you exuberantly toward success. *Yes!*

"Just say yes" to experiences that take you away from the crowd. Standing out and on your own is what makes a person transition from ordinary to extraordinary. Be like the great Barbara Jordan said in 1974 when she made her mark during the Watergate impeachment hearings, "I never intended to be a run-of-the-mill person."

Not getting offers from high-powered law firms (as would be the case today) after obtaining her law degree in 1959 from Boston University, and having to begin her law practice from her parents' dining room in Houston, Texas, Jordan could have felt discouraged. But her spirit said, "Yes, I will succeed as an attorney." After two unsuccessful runs (in 1962 and 1964) for the Texas House of Representatives, she could have given up her quest for public office with a "Why bother again?" attitude. But because she said "Yes" to trying a third time, she won an even higher post in 1966—a seat in the Texas Senate. Six years later, she said yes to running for political office again against far greater odds—and she made history by becoming a United States congressional representative from Texas.

Even after leaving Congress in 1978, Barbara Jordan kept her positive spirit. Confined to a wheelchair, her powerful voice resonated loud and clear in advocating for the citizenship of children born in the United States to undocumented immigrants. She could have said, "Now that my health has declined, I will say no to public life." But thankfully for all of us, positive thinking prevailed.

When you have a fighting spirit like Barbara Jordan had until her death in 1996, it talks back to the negative. It takes no stuff. Being positive is a nonviolent winner.

You are actually at *your* strongest when you just say yes to your own inner light—even when other people can't see it. You can't measure your inner strength by the approval you get from other people. Satisfaction comes from doing what you know is right for *you*. Don't wait for others to give you permission to search your own soul and act on what you find. When life takes you in a positive direction, just go on with it.

At a lecture given by spiritual teacher and author Marianne Williamson, someone asked her, "How can I stay positive?" Her answer surprised me.

"Look at the Crucifixion, but don't dwell on it," she said, explaining that the victory lies within the Resurrection. "We have to focus on our problems to face them, but we can't dwell there. Those of us interested in spiritual and political activism hold on to spiritualism even in the face of negativity. Our spiritual activism has to come from a loving and cheerful place."

AFFIRMATIONS

Positive thinking is what I call "affirmative self-talk." Affirmations are one kind of self-talk that can help you propel yourself in a positive direction. Not just the domain of gurus and New Age devotees, affirmations can be of your own invention. As a matter of fact, you may practice the habit of encouraging yourself with repeated empowering thoughts without even identifying it as such.

The "cool jazz" radio station in my area often plays the song by Des'ree Martin called "You Gotta Be." Even though the song is a few years old now, I imagine that it still gets regular airplay because of its positive message. I once heard the British singer say in a TV interview that before she got a hit it had been very difficult to get her music career off the ground. She had to do something to stay positive about it, so she began to place affirmations on the mirror in her bathroom.

Those affirmations became the basis for the lyrics of her first big hit. Do you have your own affirmations that keep you positive?

Pull out your journal and write down some affirmations. Remember to keep it positive and don't use words that involve lack of any kind, i.e., no, never, etc.

OPTIMISM

When you begin to live with positive thinking, you become an optimist! I love that proverbial question, "Do you see the glass as half empty or half full?" It's like the litmus test for how you see the world. Optimists have a tendency to hope for the best. That doesn't mean they hope for the best *sometimes*. It means that in all likelihood, they hope for the best all the time. Optimism has become an element of their character, a part of their disposition.

Optimists always anticipate a positive outcome. In an uncertain situation, a person who views life with optimism will believe good things will happen. She will act upon her belief, as it says in Psalm 23, that "surely goodness and mercy shall follow [her] all the days of [her] life." It's her basic instinct.

We all have plenty of opportunities to cultivate and practice optimism. Each day, there are times when we can make a conscious effort to imagine a "full" outcome, instead of an "empty" one. I remember, for example, when I was planning for my daughter's high school graduation. Her school had sent home a notice saying that if the June weather was good, the ceremony would be held outside on the school's lawn, and there was no limit to the number of friends and family we would be allowed to invite. If, however, it should rain that day, we would be given only four tickets. With relatives considering driving or flying in from out of town for the graduation, I could have been pessimistic and told them not to bother to make the trip because it might rain. The pessimistic point of view is a strong one—it was the first reaction I had.

But I was determined to be an optimist. Why? Because I wanted my daughter's graduation to be a special day for her, not one spoiled by pessimism. I had a vested interest in being optimistic—and no interest in giving power to the negative thoughts. With that in mind I gave myself a good talking to: *It's likely that it will be sunny and beautiful in June. And even if it does rain and everyone cannot attend the ceremony, we will plan a nice party at home afterward and celebrate there.*

It turned out to be a lovely, sunny day. And the weather—and my worry—was soon forgotten. But the memories of Anique's joy at sharing that day among her "village" of extended family will endure.

Optimism may not come easy: It takes work. But it is worth the effort. Don't get mad at yourself for entertaining negative thoughts. That's natural. Just don't act on them.

Instead of wallowing in your pessimism, use that energy to let your mind give rise to the possibilities for the best outcome. Try asking yourself the questions that worked for me:

- What could be the best thing that could happen in your situation?

- What can you do to aggressively turn your outlook inside out?

- What steps can you take to change your outcome?

- Even if the situation is out of your control, how can you make the best of it?

Believe me, you'll *feel* optimistic just by giving yourself this kind of pep talk. And that's the first step to changing your thought pattern to the positive.

HOPE

Hope is a cousin of optimism. With optimism, you hope for the best. With hope, you have desires with the expectation that they will be fulfilled.

In her poem "Still I Rise," poet Maya Angelou wrote "I am the dream and the hope of the slave." Her words give us inspiration because they illustrate that having hope is an ancient practice, and they prove that there is victory in hope. What a powerful force it is!

We can have hope when we feel we have nothing else. At our lowest points, we can gather the hope for a better day. Hope heals.

Like the most positive of thoughts, hope keeps us hanging on to our highest expectations. When you hope for something positive to happen, you feel full with that spirit. In other words, you feel full of hope—or hopeful.

So don't lose hope. Hang on to it. Keep it close, nurture it, and cherish it.

GREAT EXPECTATIONS

Like having high hopes, having high expectations gives you an investment in a positive outcome. When you expect great things to happen, even the anticipation of those events gives you joy. And of course, the state of joy is one of the highest forms of positivity.

When a woman gives birth to a child, she has great expectations for that infant's life. New birth is unencumbered by the problems and roadblocks of life. The path is wide open for great things to happen.

That is how we can think of great expectations, as a wide open pathway to success, joy, and our purpose. We *can* give new birth to ideas that move us forward. We *can* have great expectations of ourselves, our families, our jobs—then back it up with great works.

Too often, people fall into the trap of the low expectations that parents, teachers, employers, or our society have of them. For example, many years ago in Kansas, there was an attorney who was hired at a law firm, but given few assignments. The partners, who were white, had low expectations of the performance of this young African American, and so they gave him little work and few cases to litigate.

Fortunately, though, this person had higher expectations for himself. He hadn't struggled to pay for law school, just to sit back now. He had hoped to continue to struggle to help those who needed legal aid. He had anticipated using the law to become an advocate for the disenfranchised. He believed he was a person who could make a difference and allowed that thought to bolster his courage. As a result, he was able to leave that firm and move to another town, another state, and another law office, one that had higher expectations of him—his own. Finally free to follow his own vision, he became not only a respected attorney, but the first black state legislator from his city, and ultimately a district court judge. In the face of segregation and discrimination, which could have given him reason to have low or even no expectations, he held on to his own great expectations. I must admit that I am proud to say that this person was my father.

VISUALIZATION

You've got to *see* your vision, dream, or goal in your mind first. Like a painter, you have to visualize what the blank canvas can look like before you start on the masterpiece.

Visualization is very effective. It's one of my favorite ways to stay motivated and on track. It can also serve as a stress buster.

Before I had ever written a word of my first book, I visualized what it would be like to be an author. To get an accurate picture, I used every opportunity to attend book parties, book readings, and signings. Then I visualized myself on a book tour, I saw myself meeting new people. The magazines *Publishers Weekly, Writer's Digest,* and *Quarterly Black Review* became my blueprints. In reading about successful writers, I learned what it would take to become a published author.

When I felt down and desolate at the computer night after late, late

night, wondering if I had gotten myself in far deeper water than I co.
stand up in, I would visualize the end result. When it seemed as though
I would never finish the 400 pages I had been contracted to do, I would
indulge myself in my dream. Refreshed, as if I'd taken a quick nap, I
could then get back to work.

That's what visualization is—it's having a dream with your eyes wide
open. You could call it daydreaming, but visualization is not random. It is
purposeful and targeted. It is not the result of boredom. It is the dreaming of the wild and ready. You dream it, then you do it. Here's how:

- *Think of your goal.* Differentiate this thought from all others by
  writing down what it is you want to do. Get a notebook that you use
  only for this purpose. Say, for example, you want to go back to school
  to earn your college degree. You might write on page one "Back to
  School" in big letters. Then inside, jot down anything you think of
  that supports your goal. What course of study do you want to pursue?
  Why do you want to do it? How will it help you? What school would
  you like to attend?

- *Start by envisioning the end.* To visualize yourself doing whatever it
  is you desire, get catalogs, or photographs, illustrations, or other visual aids. Imagine yourself walking on that same lawn of the college
  that you see in the catalog. In your mind, look at the photo you will
  one day have of yourself with a cap and gown on. Imagine where that
  photo will be placed in your home. Think of how good you'll feel.

- *Imagine.* Use mental imagery to see yourself in full positivity—doing
  what it is you want to do for the highest good. Imagine yourself as
  your best ultimate self.

- *Get started.* If you find yourself dreaming more than *doing,* use this
  rule of thumb: For every visualization you indulge in, do two concrete
  things to get closer to your goal.

ul people are those who are the most flexible. They
_aight and narrow road. There's a detour here, a broken
_ there, and potholes everywhere. The signs are hard to read, or not
there at all.

You have to stay positive, knowing that you'll still get to your destination. When you are flexible, you bend but you don't break. And if you
realize that flexibility is required, then you won't catch an attitude, or
curse someone out when you come to that proverbial brick wall. You'll
just say, "Oh, I figured there would be a brick wall on my path somewhere! Now let me see how to get around it."

My friend Marlene F. Watson, who is a psychologist, says that flexibility is a major element of success and positive thinking. "In my private practice as a therapist, when I see people who are inflexible, I tell
them that flexibility is a cornerstone of success. You must have the ability to see the open door behind the closed door. Explore options. Don't
get stuck if your ideal plan doesn't work—look for what will work. Just
remember the old saying, 'It's a poor rat that only has one hole.'"

Speaking of rats, recently I happened to listen to an audio book of
the bestseller *Who Moved My Cheese?* Written by the author of *The
One-Minute Manager,* Dr. Spencer Johnson, *Who Moved My Cheese?* is
a fable about four kinds of mice, two who "sniff" and "scurry" after
change, and two who "hem" and "haw" about it. The day after I listened
to the tape, I went to a gathering where several people were buzzing
about the book. "Which one did you relate to?" people asked each other.
"Were you the one who adapts to change, or the one who resists it?"
Without giving the entire plot away, I'll tell you that one of the maxims of
the book is "Adapt to change quickly." The quicker you let go of the old
cheese, the sooner you can enjoy the new cheese.

Whether the cheese in your life is represented by your job, your relationships, or your personal goals, flexibility is the positive energy we
can use in the face of change.

ACHIEVEMENT

Positive thinking gives birth to great achievement, and achievement breeds a positive attitude. So which comes first? They go hand in hand.

As the saying goes, "Whatever you conceive, you can achieve, if you only believe." The positive thoughts you give birth to, that you nurture and bring to life, can make you feel empowered. You can make them happen if you only believe that they *can* happen. If you don't believe they can, who else will? And who else should feel more strongly about your own plans and goals than you? No one.

Of course, not everything we achieve is of our own doing. There is group achievement, there is teamwork, organization, the spirit of the village. Pulling together for a common goal can bring a lifetime of positive memories. Singing in a church choir, playing in a school band, performing in an ensemble cast, dancing with the troop, coaching a team of athletes, operating with the surgical staff—these are all positive experiences that can lead to great achievement. However, someone has to take the lead. Someone has to articulate the vision and the goal to the others. And if you are positive in your thoughts about the ultimate outcome, then that person could be you.

As Martin Luther King, Jr., said on many an occasion, "Be a drum major." In the taped sermon played at his funeral, King said he wanted to be remembered as a "drum major for justice." Think of the image of drum majors jammin' at a football game. Consider the Grambling College half-time program, with the high-hatted drum major—out front, strutting, lively, high-steppin', proud.

That's what it takes sometimes to get folks behind you in order to win the game. It takes a lot of out-front high-steppin'. You may find yourself leading the cheers, rallying the troops, getting the crowd stirred up. All for the goal, the high score, the achievement of winning. You can't win lying down. The winning attitude is an active one. It's not passive, it's positive. And that positive frame of mind leads to achievement.

HAPPINESS

Of course, if you are happy, you will feel positive. But so often, we keep happiness at bay. Although negative things happen to make us sad or angry or upset, we can't let those feelings become our pervasive mind-set. No suffering lasts forever. The problems we had at fourteen are rarely what we deal with at forty-one. We can find comfort in knowing "this too shall pass."

One day I read in the popular pamphlet *Our Daily Bread* about a "set point" theory of happiness. David Lykken, an emeritus professor at the University of Minnesota, contends that after dramatic events like the sorrow of losing a loved one or the thrill of moving into a dream home, most people return to their previous level of happiness within six months to a year. He calls that original reference point of happiness their "set point."

Unfortunately, for many of us the set point is much too low. We wonder how we can return to happiness when we didn't have it previously. We wait for others to make us happy. Songs express how "you make me so very happy" and that we should "make someone happy." This perpetuates the myth that happiness is something outside of us, that we have to give it or get it—that it's not something within ourselves that we can tap into.

Our happiness is our birthright. Psalm 4:7 says "You have put gladness in my heart." If we look to what is in our hearts, we'll find that happiness isn't something that *happens* to us. It is always there inside us.

I have some friends who are happy people. That doesn't mean that they don't experience sad or sorrowful things; it's that they know how to put those things in the perspective of the abundant joy in their lives. I saw one friend at a funeral recently, and remarkably, the first thing she said was "Oh, I am so happy to see you!" She was grieving, but that didn't stop her from acknowledging that her life was going on, and that there were momentary joys still in it. She has a gladness in her heart that carries her through the difficult times. My friend knows that when you are smiling, you can't also be crying.

When we wait for others to make us happy, we could wait forever! We say, "I'll be happy if I could just . . ." Fill in the blank: . . . find a

man, . . . get a big house, . . . drive a certain car, . . . quit my job. Whatever it is, it is always some exterior thing. The gladness in your heart is
an interior thing.

Gospel singer Yolanda Adams is a happy person. I asked her point-
blank in a NiaOnline interview, "Are you happy?"

"Yes," she said. "And it's so amazing that there are so few people who
say they are really happy. My husband and I have this conversation all
the time about being happy where we are. Before all the big money
came, before the big record deals came, before all of this fame came—
I was a happy person. I was happy with *me*.

"I was raised to know no one can make you happy. You have to be
happy within yourself. When you know who you are . . . when you have
the love of family, the love of friends, and the love of God in your
heart—there's no reason to be unhappy. You have the stuff money can't
buy. Of course, money does really wonderful things once you know who
you are. But when you don't know who you are, then money becomes
the substitute for joy, for happiness, for peace.

"I learned this from my mom, from my grandmother. There's something about wonderful upbringing, to have that foundation. I'm just
grateful that I had it."

How do you tap into it? First, like Yolanda, you have to give importance to the happiness you have. Don't take for granted the love of family, shelter from the elements, safety from crime. Don't wait for
happiness to come to you. Seek it out on your own.

I came across a community of "happy people," so to speak. I should
say, a *cyber*community of happy people. I heard or read about The Secret Society of Happy People. On its Web site (*www.sohp.com*) there are
ways to join the club or start your own. The society was formed in 1998
to encourage the expression of happiness and discourage parade raining
(parade rainers are described as those people who don't want to hear
your happy news). "Somewhere between *The Ed Sullivan Show* and *The
Jerry Springer Show,* talking about being happy became politically incorrect," states Pam Johnson, the society's founder, who has even espoused
happiness on the TV show *Politically Incorrect*. "We're more comfortable airing our dirty laundry than telling people we've had a happy moment." She goes on to say on her site that "happiness is contagious and

when more people talk about happy events and moments, it will be chic for everyone to do it." Just like misery loves company, so does happiness—so why not attract the company of happy, positive people, instead of *les misérables?* Happiness is a state of grace. Enjoy it.

I know one young woman in her early thirties who is waiting to get married before she buys a home. She does not have a man in her life, but she does make a sizable salary, enough to pay a mortgage as easily as she now pays rent. Although she obsesses about having a house, she is putting off her happiness.

We have a mutual friend in her fifties who bought a home when she was single and in her thirties. She has not married, but that has not stopped her from fulfilling her dream of enjoying many years in a lovely home with a beautiful garden. Guess which woman is the happiest?

Make a list of what keeps you happy inside. Leave off any material things. Is it a smile on your child's face? Is it the sand in your toes on a sunny beach? How about your grandma's hugs, sweet memories of childhood, the joke you just made up? Does keeping a journal give you joy? When your favorite sports team wins, are you glad?

It is not only the major events of weddings, births, graduations, promotions, and raises that can bring us pleasure. Rather it is the constant chain of small blessings that keep us living in bliss and happiness.

KARMA

You reap what you sow. What goes around, comes around. That's how we usually think of karma. If you do something bad, something bad will come back to you.

Actually, karma is just simply cause and effect. It could be negative, but it just as well could be positive. Why not live your life with the assumption that your good deeds will come back to you, that the good you give is what you will receive? Put a positive spin on it. Then live it.

Positive karma is a righteous life-force that results in constructive energy. Let's compare positive with negative karma:

> *Negative karma*: Punishment and revenge
> *Positive karma*: Justice and reward

Negative karma: Lies and dishonesty
Positive karma: Truth and integrity

Negative karma: Manipulation and control
Positive karma: Respect and free-spiritedness

Negative karma: Aggressiveness and arrogance
Positive karma: Assertiveness and humility

Negative karma: Selfishness and greed
Positive karma: Caring and compassion

Negative karma: Skepticism and mistrust
Positive karma: Belief and faith

Whether or not you have negative or positive karma all begins with your negative or positive thoughts. I believe it is impossible to find your ultimate purpose while operating under negative karma, so keep your karma on the positive. Perform an act of kindness and then expect good things.

PARTY FOR A PURPOSE

Celebration gives us joy and allows us to honor our triumphs. Throwing a party is a fun way to acknowledge a happy occasion. Baby showers, birthdays, anniversaries, and other celebrations take us away from our daily concerns and feed the spirit. Planning a party with a positive purpose is not only good for you, but can benefit others.

Ask black folks in major urban cities if they've heard of "First Friday," and I bet most will say yes. The claim to the name of the popular networking events across the country, has been laid by Gloria Buck, who says she started the first event called "First Friday" in Newark, New Jersey, in 1987. "Friends from Washington, D.C., moved to the area and asked, 'Where do the professional people come together?'" she explains. Since there wasn't any such place, she started a monthly event for networking and socializing among African American professionals over age thirty.

On a recent First Friday in the new millennium, I overheard a dermatologist talking with an ob-gyn. In the VIP room, where my book sign-ing was being held, the dermatologist's lawyer husband held a conver-sation with a flight attendant. In previous years, one might have seen the mayor of Newark holding court in that same chamber. Downstairs on the dance floor, accountants boogied with actors, and hairstylists shared laughs with sales execs.

More than just a meet-and-greet, this was a party for a purpose. Buck says, "In the beginning, we sent out engraved invitations, so we've always drawn an upscale crowd." At one point, that crowd grew to over one thousand people and the event had to be held at the Newark Air-port Marriott. The idea of networking and de-stressing on a Friday night caught on in other cities, too. "Other folks have now started Black Fri-days, Second Fridays, and Last Fridays," Buck continues with amuse-ment. She has now distinguished her events by having a separate room in which revelers can relax and hear an author read, have their blood pressure checked, or see a fitness demonstration, like the one a repre-sentative from the local YWCA presented the night I was there.

"People over thirty are always looking for places without all the young people," Buck says, explaining her success at pulling off monthly parties for a purpose. "I liked putting people together, and filling a need."

That is the secret to a successful party or any other positive en-deavor. If you fill a need, people will come.

I had the need to dance recently. My husband, Reggie, and I had been working hard 24/7, when we went to church one Sunday and heard that the congregation would be giving an oldies-but-goodies dance on the upcoming weekend. Not sure if we could attend, we bought tick-ets just to support the fund-raising effort. By the time Friday night rolled around, our daughter had told us that she thought she would stay home and not accompany us to dinner because "you two seem to need a night out together." Now, you know things are getting bad when your own child feels the need to tell her parents to go out on a date!

We went to dinner at our favorite Italian restaurant, then remem-bering the dance, we decided to just pop in. Well, when we got there James Brown was blasting from the Women's Club! A formerly conser-vative organization that over the years has allowed their facility to be rented out, the women of the club probably couldn't have imagined that

J.B. would ever be calling out to Maceo to "give the drummer some!" in their pristine palace. But getting out of the car and hearing James and the Famous Flames "Talking Loud and Saying Nothin' " was all Reg and I needed to enter the hall dancing.

At church the following Sunday, Rev. Phyllis Crichlow, who had been seen on the dance floor herself, announced that the party had raised over $2,000. Not bad for a little church that just wanted to have some fun while fund-raising.

Sly and the Family Stone sang "I Want to Take You Higher." Well, any family with a child old enough to throw a party can teach that teenager how to take it to a higher level—and I don't mean with drugs or alcohol, either. My teenage daughter's teen group had a Valentine's Dance at which they raised money for a children's charity. Charging eight dollars and allowing each teen of the group of forty to sell five tickets, they grossed $1,600, and after they covered the costs of the hall rental and the DJ, they still had over $600 to give to the nonprofit organization that provides services to children of homeless families. Teaching a child to party with a purpose is an easy way to foster a caring attitude and a positive spirit of giving back to the community. The message: You don't have to be grown to do something good for someone else. When you act with purpose, you feel good, too.

HUMOR

Why do people laugh? "Because it's in them," said Richard Pryor in a Comedy Central special. "And you say something that touches them and they have to let it out. The biggest compliment to me is when I see people doubled over."

When Richard Pryor was at his peak, I was one of those people who was doubled over often. I knew that laughing at his jokes had a positive effect on me, but little did I know that humor can lower stress, boost the immune system, and reduce blood pressure. Humor has a way of strengthening the immune system by boosting the levels of body chemicals that fight cancer and other diseases. You don't even have to be laughing at something happening at the moment for humor to work its magic on you; anticipating or remembering something humorous is equally beneficial. And just keeping a smile on your face, studies show, gives you a more upbeat outlook on life.

"Laugh therapy" has been known to help people in pain. That may be the origin of the saying "Laughter is the best medicine." And as I mentioned before, it's hard to cry when you are busy laughing. Langston Hughes, the great poet and humorist, may have known that, which is why he wrote a book of humorous short stories called *Laughing to Keep from Crying.*

Seeing the humor in situations from the silly to the serious is a positive, soulful secret in a wholesome, successful life. Here are some ways to infuse a laugh line into your daily dealings:

Keep a joke book. Whenever you hear a funny saying, riddle, or joke, jot it down. Get a pocket-size blank book in which to keep humorous ruminations only.

Buy a book of humor. Most bookstores have a humor section full of funny books, from comic strips to comedian memoirs.

Get it on video. Like bookstores, video stores always have a particular shelf in the store for comedies. Rent a variety of fun videos, but buy your favorite to keep at home in case you need an emergency pick-me-up.

Cultivate a sense of humor. Have a hard time figuring out what's so funny? Make a greater effort to identify your funny bone. Maybe Shakespeare plays are more enjoyable humor for you than Chris Rock's stand-up routine. Identify what tickles your fancy—and tickle it often!

Have funny friends. Just about everyone has a friend who is forever making you say, "That woman (or guy) is *crazy!*" As a child, I had a young neighbor who was always full of fun and kept our family in stitches. Welcome in our home anytime, he often started our days off in good humor showing up for breakfast before school. Many years later, my husband's aunt was the person to call if you wanted a good laugh. She kept us rolling on the floor with her tall tales. If you have a funny friend, you know who to call when you need the "best medicine."

Don't take yourself so seriously. For some of us, it's hard to laugh *at* ourselves. But I have noticed that most of the funniest comedians are those who laugh at their own shortcomings or failures. Richard Pryor's humor was often self-deprecating—like when he told the story of how he set himself on fire! The great, late Moms Mabley made fun of herself when she said things like, "There's nothing an old man can do for me—except tell me where to find a young man!" Joan Rivers pokes fun at her own well-known shopping habits when she exclaims, "If the shoe fits, buy it!"

❧ *Your Positivity Journal** ❧

I know I live with a positive purpose because:

These are the positive people in my life that I call on when I need an "upper" (list names and phone numbers):

When I use visualization, I see myself in the future doing . . .

When I think of using humor to stay positive, I remember the time it worked when . . .

*If you prefer not to write in this book, make a copy of this page or write in the journal you have been using for previous chapters.

$\mathscr{O}$PTIMUM HEALTH

Allow me to get straight to the point: It's hard to have ultimate success without optimum health. Physical and mental fitness give us the strength to overcome the obstacles we often face on the road to reaching our potential and purpose. It's difficult to imagine achieving much when we are sick and tired. Endurance, whether for a foot race or life's race, is necessary to win. If Oprah Winfrey were to get sick, what would happen to her show? How could Denzel Washington give an Oscar-winning performance while feeling "blah?" How can you ace that test, keep up with your toddler, compete for that promotion—just keep on keeping on—if you're not in top shape?

To get in optimum shape, we have to make a commitment to health and fitness. To succeed in *anything*, we have to have commitment. A passion for the purpose and a commitment to the cause go hand in hand. Often the journey to getting where we want to go is so daunting, so difficult, so plain hard that if we aren't 100 percent committed, it just won't happen. We have to be serious about wanting the success. We can't half-step. Either you're committed to reaching your full potential or you ain't.

In most areas of our lives, commitment is required. If you love someone, it's pretty certain that eventually that person will want to see evidence of your commitment. An "I love you" here, an introduction to Mama there. A ring maybe, a marriage license, perhaps.

In business, signing a contract signifies commitment to an agreement. Then, the way we fulfill our end of the agreement becomes a testimony to our competence and professionalism. Positive or negative assessments of us are made as a result of how we follow through on commitments we have made. We should commit ourselves to achieving our personal goals with the same seriousness we give to business contracts. We should create a personal contract and sign it. Follow through: Carry out the agreement you made with yourself. Agree to commit to doing what it takes to have a healthy lifestyle of good nutrition, regular exercise, and disease-preventive habits.

In several surveys of public attitudes that I've come across, people equate success with good health. And for good reason. Our health is our wealth.

I once heard about a man who won the lottery in Washington State. Unfortunately, he was in ill health, and died before he could enjoy it. Which do you think he would have preferred, to have his health—and a longer life—or the wealth? Of course, anyone would want both, but my point is that health is priceless. And you know the old adage about money: You can't take it with you.

What's the most common refrain of expectant parents when asked, "Do you want a boy or girl?"

Answer: "It doesn't matter, as long as it's healthy."

What do most people on the planet want more than wealth? Answer: health.

No matter who we are, from womb to tomb we want optimum health. Yet we tend to value it most when we don't have it. And when we do have it, especially when we're young and kickin', we often take it for granted and indulge in the risky behaviors of smoking, drinking, drugging, overeating, and underexercising. Add racism, stress, and societal pressures to the mix and it's no wonder our wondrous bodies break down.

I want you to arm yourself to become stronger than the negative influences that surround us. With a positive, practical, and personal attitude, you can empower yourself to take control of your health. If you are strong and fit, you will glow with good health, you'll choose whole and healthy relationships, and you'll learn to love the unique person that you are. In doing that, you will reach your purpose.

When *Heart & Soul* was launched, the editorial team and I developed a mission statement comprising principles that the magazine would stand for and that each reader could benefit from. We were aided in this effort by our editorial director at the time, Mark Bricklin, the former editor of *Prevention* magazine. Now, several years later, I still follow this philosophy and carry the ideas into every article I write, book I publish, and speech I deliver. More important, it defines my own way of living and guides my family's lifestyle in the pursuit of good health. Feel free to tweak it so it suits your own life.

The ideas that make up this philosophy are interconnected—they work best when applied together to achieve your optimal well-being. Many of the healthy habits that follow will seem like common sense to you—and they are. But what is common sense is not always common practice. With motivation and inspiration, however, you can live a healthier life!

💗 *Seven Soulful Secrets of* 💗 *Commitment to Health and Happiness*

People who enjoy the best of health, and who are most content with themselves and the world around them, have a lifestyle that includes many of the following traits.

1. *Practice positive living.* Are you an optimist or a pessimist? People who overcome odds and most often succeed maintain a healthy outlook. Health is the foundation upon which all other positive aspects of life depend. Living positively includes having a strong sense of spirituality, of tranquillity, of purpose in life, of self-esteem, and most important, of love and happiness (if you don't believe me, ask Al Green; his mantra still holds!). With the psychological energy of positive living, even the toughest challenge is easier to meet. See Chapter Four for more information on positivity.

2. *Commit to healthy habits.* Make a pact with yourself to abstain from smoking and from abusing alcohol or other substances. Also commit to safer sex, better sleep habits, and other simple health and safety precautions, like installing smoke detectors in your house and changing the batteries once a year (for example, in October, which is Fire Safety Month). Another easy healthy practice is to get in the habit of always using a seat belt. This may seem like a commonsense suggestion, but unfortunately, seat belt usage by African Americans is more than 10 percent below the national average, which may contribute to the fact that motor vehicle crashes are the leading cause of death for African American children under age fourteen. And don't forget to strap Baby in the backseat. *Never, ever* allow a child to sit on someone's lap in the front seat. When my daughter was a youngster, I made her think the backseat was a special place for good little girls. Child psychology works! (Special note to urban dwellers: Remember to fasten your seat belt in a taxi, too.)

3. *Be an eternal student of good nutrition.* Healthy people see food as fuel for the body and soul. They study the effects of certain foods on the body—and not only when they have bad reactions to something, like lactose intolerance or allergies. They find out what foods contain what vitamins, and they examine and consider the pros and cons of ingredients on food labels. Take a tip from them and refrain from using food as recreation or an antidote for stress. Create a healthier lifestyle. Nourish your body with foods low in fat, and eat more vegetables, beans, fruits, and whole grains. Make these, not meat, the center of your meals.

4. *Make physical fitness a priority.* Commit to regular exercise. All the evidence suggests that keeping fit is not just a healthy bonus but a vital necessity. And in keeping with the research, fitness experts suggest daily, moderate exercise—like walking—over high-impact sports.

5. *Obtain and/or maintain a healthy weight.* Steer away from "diets," and stress conscious control overeating habits. Couple good nutrition with regular exercise to achieve a normal, healthy weight. This may be a benefit for vanity, but more important, it can prevent heart dis-

ease, hypertension, and diabetes—all life-threatening diseases that African Americans, in particular, are more prone to than other Americans.

6. *Take control of your health care.* Be proactive in seeking preventive care. It's not just about shots and checkups; it also means actively participating in your relationship with your doctor, dentist, and other health practitioners—and being an advocate for high-quality health care for everyone.

7. *Pursue healthy relationships.* Make the people you love a priority. Good love is what we all need and deserve—as a matter of fact, is there any other *real* love? Creating a cocoon of loving ties around you is important work. Strong relationships are a vital aspect of emotional and physical health. Also, because of pervasive domestic violence, we must consider our health when we select a partner. The choices we make in relationships can have effects on other areas of our lives. When we commit to maintaining caring, supportive bonds with our mate, family members, and friends, when we feel the benefits of their trust and loyalty in return, we feel its all worth the effort.

To make the planet a better place, we need everyone to be at her/his best. Our society needs you to be strong and healthy. If you take care of your body, you'll be able to take care of business. Your family needs you; the community needs you. *You* need *you* to be healthy and happy. With a commitment to getting there, you can make it happen.

❦ *From Quick Fix to the Lifestyle Mix!* ❦

With all the information we're constantly bombarded with about health and fitness, it's no wonder people are confused about what's good for them. You hear one thing from your doctor, learn something else from a TV commercial, and read yet a third conflicting "fact" in the newspaper. Then your girlfriend mentions a natural remedy that everyone is talking about, but your sister says that it has harmful side effects, and when you turn on the radio you hear on the news that the remedy hasn't received FDA approval anyway. All this while you're trying to juggle eating three square meals a day, getting your children to take their vitamins, and wondering if your father has ever had a prostate exam.

To help make health and fitness less of a chore, I find it helpful to make it part of my lifestyle. Instead of chasing quick fixes based on the latest fads, if you incorporate the routines and habits of healthy living into everything you do, better health will come more naturally to you. And when it becomes second nature, it's less of a hassle.

I speak from personal experience when I say you can incorporate healthy habits into your life. When I was eighteen years old, I hadn't thought too much about the good or bad effects of food or exercise on my body or well-being. Heck, when you are eighteen, you feel good and you think you're going to continue to feel good forever—no matter what you do.

Sure, some "politically correct" movements had a minor effect on people like me. For example, it just wasn't cool to eat pork. During the politically charged sixties, some black radicals believed that we shouldn't eat "swine," especially those parts of that unsanitary animal, like the feet and the intestines, that our enslaved ancestors had been given as morsels left over after the oppressor's family had taken the more choice cuts.

Then some animal-rights advocates began to persuade people not to eat any meat at all. Just like the antifur activists, these folks felt that the consumption of meat amounted to cruelty to animals. And apparently, some people still feel this way. "I don't eat *animals*," I heard an actress say recently on a sitcom.

But just as peer pressure can have a negative effect on a young mind, being around someone doing something positive can turn a person in a positive direction. After gaining my "freshman fifteen," those fifteen extra pounds that crept up on me during my first year of college from eating junk food, fast food, and fattening food, I started dating a vegetarian. When I decided to use him as a good model and eat more vegetables, those extra pounds came off and stayed off. I not only looked better, I felt better too.

Previously, my college roommates and I would go to the takeout joint for lunch and order burgers, fries, and shakes, or big submarine sandwiches that were larger than we needed to eat, but we didn't want to waste what little money we had. Then for dinner, we would go to the nearby hospital's cafeteria for the all-you-can-eat soul-food meals and pig out. For hours after our meal, we would sit around and complain about how full we felt. "I feel like such a pig!" someone would inevitably whine. And of course, it never occurred to us to take a run around the school's track to work it off.

When I stopped eating meat and began to study which foods were good for my body, I noticed that not only did my brain feel enlightened but my body felt lighter.

I did have to overcome the skepticism of those who weren't with me on that vegetarian wavelength. "*You* are not going to eat this good ol' sausage?" my father asked me the Christmas I brought my boyfriend home from school and my mother served a big spread of home-cooked food for Sunday brunch. When I answered "No, thank you," he got pretty hysterical.

And people my own age made it no easier. "Are you still into that vegetarian thang?" classmates would ask. "I'm not just *into* it, it's part of my lifestyle." Before I changed my eating habits, rather than letting nutritional concerns dictate what I ate, I pretty much ate anything that tasted good to me. Taste was really the only consideration. Now I know that if you are in the habit of following your taste buds alone, you can eat a lot of very tasty meals on your way to obesity, heart disease, diabetes, cancer, and any number of other health problems.

So I got in the *habit* of eating well, and I didn't have to give up flavor to do it. It became my lifestyle to eat less meat and more fish. I acquired a taste for eggplant, stir-fried vegetables, and international cuisine. I got as close to my new passion as "brown on rice"—as I began eating brown rice and brown bread, and using whole wheat flour and soy margarine.

Eating better, refraining from bad habits like smoking and drinking, taking dance class and later tennis, and then power walking has kept my body in pretty good shape these last twenty-five years.

So I learned through trial and error some ways to stay healthy and fit. And from the research I've done on how to maintain a strong mind, body, and spirit, it all comes down to three pretty simple ways to keep it all together:

The Three-Part Harmony of Health

- Good nutrition

- Frequent exercise

- Healthy habits

Now doesn't that sound easy? Well, really it is just common sense. Most of us know the things we can do to be at our optimum health, but we just don't put them into common practice. So, to help motivate you, here are some tips, information, and—I hope—inspiration to get you committed to leading a better lifestyle—and to keep you at your ultimate, healthy self.

❦ Good Nutrition ❦

Give a Dish a Makeover

If it's healthy food, it must taste bland, right?

Well, be your own judge. How do collard greens, sweet potatoes, chicken, and peach cobbler sound to you? Umm-umm, good? They sound good to me, too, and they are "soul foods" that I was raised on and that are integral parts of African American cuisine. The thing to realize about these foods, however, is that they can be prepared in myriad ways. It's not that the foods themselves are bad for us, indeed they can be good for us. Greens, for example, are high in vitamins A and C, and in calcium, iron, and potassium, and low in calories and fat. For optimal nutrition, prepare them with herbs, spices, and seasonings, rather than in the traditional ways with ham hocks or fatback. Want to try preparing them in a new way? Instead of boiling them for *hours* in the conventional way, boil kale, for instance, for fifteen minutes, then stir-fry it with onions and garlic.

I was almost thirty years old before I knew that you could bake a yam, just like you do a regular, white potato. Having always eaten—and loved—*candied* yams, it never occurred to me to prepare them any other way. Experimentation is the best way to discover nutritious ways to cook foods. Instead of always having candied yams, try baked yams some-times. That doesn't mean you have to deny yourself the foods you like. Just mix it up. Moderation is the key to just about anything. If you save your mama's delicious candied yam recipe for special occasions, soon the dish will indeed become more special.

Other food makeovers:

- Chicken

    Before: fried, fried, and fried some more

    After: baked, stir-fried, grilled, skinless

- Pizza

    Before: pepperoni, sausage

    After: peppers, onions, mushrooms

- Peaches

    Before: baked in a cobbler with lots of sugary syrup

    After: freshly sliced pieces served with vanilla yogurt

You can also makeover your entire meal plan. Here are some sug-gestions on how to take your meals from not-so-great to great. To ease into the habit of eating right, try the following suggestions once a week, then twice, then increase the frequency until you've made it a habit:

FOR BREAKFAST

Not so great: bacon, eggs, biscuits

Better: pancakes, french toast, bagel with cream cheese

Best: whole grain cereal with fruit

For a Snack When You Get to Work

Not so great: coffee and a donut

Better: tea and a low-fat muffin

Best: juice, an orange or apple

For Lunch

Not so great: a burger and fries

Better: a salad with chopped meat, sliced eggs, cheese, croutons and a light dressing

Best: a grilled chicken breast sandwich, without mayo

For an Afternoon Snack

Not so great: a candy bar, potato chips, or cookies

Better: crackers with peanut butter or cheese

Best: an apple, orange, banana, or sticks of carrots or celery

Your Choice of Beverage

Not so great: sodas, coffee

Better: tea, whole milk

Best: juice, water, one-percent milk

AND NOW FOR DESSERT . . .

Not so great: cake, pie, pastry, ice cream

Better: frozen yogurt, fruit sorbet

Best: mixed fresh fruit cup

ALIVE AT FIVE

If there were one thing that people could do to improve their health through their diet, what would it be? Well, the United States Surgeon General, the Centers for Disease Control and Prevention, the American Heart Association, the American Cancer Society, and the National Cancer Institute all agree on what that one thing is: *Eat more fruits and vegetables.* The goal? *Five servings a day.*

Currently, over 50 percent of Americans don't eat a piece of fruit at all during a day. And over 60 percent of us eat less than five servings of fruits and vegetables, so that means that under 40 percent of us are getting the amount needed. That's too bad, because less means more when it comes to the number of people who suffer from high blood pressure, stroke, diabetes, and cardiovascular disease.

So how can we change our mindset and make "five a day" a habit? Try this:

- *For breakfast:* have fruit with your cereal, drink juice

- *At lunch:* a salad full of dark, leafy greens, raw veggies, and beans. The next day have a fruit salad.

- When you think *"snack"* think: apple, pear, orange, or some other kind of fresh fruit

- *For dinner:* at least one vegetable on your plate, fruit for dessert

When you think of a "serving," think like this:

- ¾ cup of fruit or vegetable juice

- one cup of raw spinach (i.e., to make a spinach salad)

- ½ cup of raw or cooked vegetables (to put in that salad)

- a medium-size orange, apple, or banana; half a grapefruit

- ½ cup chopped, cooked, or canned fruit

Consuming each of those servings in one day would make five a day. That's not so difficult, is it? Maybe it even sounds like your typical diet. Just be honest with yourself about whether it truly is typical for you, or whether it's more likely that you are eating on the run, grabbing fast food, or eating whatever is convenient. Try to switch the scenario so that you are most likely to eat healthfully more days than not. Then try to make it a habit of consuming five a day most of the time. Soon you'll find that even if you like foods that aren't so good for you, you'll only eat them occasionally rather than as your steady diet. Now, that will be doing something!

Another good thing about eating a better diet is that it doesn't cost much. Studies conducted by the Food Marketing Institute indicate that a large number of people feel that eating well is too expensive. There's an assumption that eating well means buying expensive food from the health-food store. Besides the fact that not everything at health-food stores cost more than other food, the foods listed above are "health foods" that can be purchased at your local supermarket. For people on limited budgets, "five a day" will cost less than fast food.

But don't just take my word for it. There are free brochures you can get from the Consumer Information Center; call for their catalog at (888) 8-PUEBLO. In addition, the National Cancer Institute and the Centers for Disease Control and Prevention have collaborated on a Web site that explains more about the national effort to eat five fruits and vegetables a day. Check it out at *www.5aday.gov.*

Don't Fight the Fiber

Your grandmother probably called it roughage. And back then you probably called it something you preferred not to eat. But fiber by any name
is food that helps your digestive system, moves your bowels, and helps
prevent little annoyances, such as hemorrhoids, and bigger bothers,
such as heart disease and colon cancer.

Government regulations require that for a food to be considered a
"good source of fiber," it must contain at least 2½ grams of fiber per serving. To claim to be a "high fiber" food, each serving must contain at least
5 grams. Nutritionists recommend that we get at least 25 to 30 grams
per day. Unfortunately, most of us consume less than 15 grams.

Not sure where to find some fiber? Here are some foods to fill up on:

- Apples

- Apricots

- Baked potato

- Barley

- Beans (red, pinto, black, garbanzo, etc.)

- Brown rice

- Figs

- Lentils

- Oat bran

- Oranges

- Peaches

- Pears

- Raisins

- Wheat bran

- Wheat germ

- Whole wheat

Please Pass (Up) the Salt

I started eating salt-free by buying no-salt potato chips. After that, I didn't want any salt on my fries. Eventually, I stopped shaking salt onto just about anything on my plate. I began to trust that the chef—or I—prepared the meal with exactly the seasonings it should have without my additional help, thank you.

Consuming too much sodium, which is 40 percent of salt, can lead to health problems. That's because it causes our bodies to retain too much water, making the heart work harder and blood pressure to rise. And as you should know, high blood pressure can cause stroke, heart attack, and kidney failure.

There are three ways we commonly consume sodium:

- Cooking with salt

- Adding salt at the table

- Eating processed fast foods

Most of the time, we only consider that salt enhances the taste of the foods we eat. But we should also consider the health cost of that taste. If you were to cut salt out of your diet right now, you might think that the foods you normally eat taste too bland. But if you cut down gradually, you'll be more likely to stick with it. Here are guidelines from the National Academy of Sciences:

Intake should be limited to 2,400 mg of sodium, or about 1¼ teaspoons of salt.

Unfortunately, most of us ingest more than that without adding a drop of salt at the table. But we can cut down by keeping in mind the following:

Seven Secrets to Cutting Down on Salt

1. Think fresh. Fruits and vegetables contain a lower amount of sodium than canned food.

2. Check the labels. Virtually all food manufacturers are required to list the sodium content per serving (so remember to do the math if you eat more than one serving.) With this information, you can add up the amount of sodium you eat and keep the 2,400 mg level under control.

3. If you do choose canned or processed foods, look for brands that claim to be "no sodium," "sodium free," "salt free," or "no salt added." These should provide less than 5 mg per serving.

4. Next best thing is "very-low-sodium" products, which mean the sodium content is 35 mg or less.

5. "Low sodium" is 140 mg or less.

6. Avoid seasonings with salt in the name, such as "seasoning salt" and "garlic salt."

7. Experiment. In rice, use allspice, basil, dill, fennel, marjoram, parsley, or saffron. On chicken, try curry powder, dill, lemon juice, dry mustard, rosemary. On fish, use basil, curry, dill, garlic, lemon juice, paprika, sage. When cooking greens, try vinegar or cayenne pepper.

The Easy Way to Eat Healthfully

As I mentioned before, it's so difficult to know what to eat, and what not to eat, what's good for you, and what'll kill ya. So to make it easy as pie— oops, I mean easy as eating an apple—I've placed the traditional groups into three categories: What you can feel free to consume generously, what you should eat in moderation, and what experts advise that you eat sparingly. In other words . . .

- *Eat a whole bunch of:* Whole wheat breads, whole-grain cereals, brown rice, pasta

  Greens, corn, carrots, peas, onions, and other vegetables

  Oranges, apples, bananas, grapes, grapefruit, melons, and other fruits

- *Eat some:* Fish, poultry, lean beef

  Dried beans, nuts

  Milk (1 percent, lactose-free, or skim), low-fat yogurt, natural cheeses

- *Be cool with:* Sweets and snacks high in sugar, fat, and salt, such as potato chips, candies, and sodas

  Any foods high in saturated fats and oils, such as bacon, sausage, chitterlings, hog maws, pig's feet—you get the picture.

Have a Snack Attack

When I was a kid the common wisdom was to eat three square meals a day. Now that advice is considered square. Today the more likely recommendation is to have several small meals or snacks throughout the day.

"Won't that make everybody fat?" you may ask. The answer is that it's not how often you eat, but *what* you eat *when* you eat.

Here's how the snack attack works: You eat more often, but you eat more healthfully. Eating small meals or snacks throughout the day keeps hunger at bay. You're more likely to keep your weight under control if you eat smaller meals more frequently than if you eat big meals less often during the day.

Here are some dos and don'ts for choosing healthy snacks:

- *Don't* go to a candy store or vending machine when you want a snack. **Do** eat more fresh fruits and raw vegetables. Try foods with whole grains.

- *Don't* assume you can tell by looking at an item how much sugar, fat, or calories it contains. **Do** read the labels and compare foods.

- *Don't* go for the same old sweets. **Do** pick up some low-fat pound cake, raisin bread or toast, fresh fruits, and dried fruits, such as apricots.

- *Don't* keep your eyes on the fries when you're craving salt. **Do** go for dry-roasted nuts (ever tried them without the salt?), sardines, or low-fat sharp cheese with whole wheat crackers.

- *Don't* pick a pack of potato chips to satisfy your desire for crunchy munchies. **Do** grab a handful of dry cereal, air-pop some corn, attack some no-salt, low-fat crackers. For heaven's sake, try a rice cake (if you think rice cakes mean blah taste, you should check them out now—they come in all kinds of yummy varieties).

- *Don't* even bother to cook. **Do** have a fresh-fruit smoothie, a tall glass of your favorite juice, a frozen juice bar (you can make your own by freezing juice in ice-cube containers), some yogurt, or applesauce.

- *Don't* forsake the foods of your childhood. **Do** give your childhood favorites a grown-up makeover. I always loved peanut butter and jelly sandwiches. But now, instead of high-cal, high-sugar jelly on white bread, I prefer a PB&J of peanut butter and apple butter on whole-grain. I ordered it from the menu at a health-food cafe years ago, and I've been saying "Yum, yum, yum" ever since.

THE ULTIMATE VITAMINS

Another age-old piece of advice you've probably heard for years is "Take your vitamins." Multivitamins are a good way to get the USDA-recommended dosages of essential vitamins and minerals. Now many health experts point out the value in certain vitamins only half-jokingly referred to as "celebrity compounds." You know how there are everyday people, and then there are celebrities, or stars? Well, vitamins have it like that, too.

The stars of the vitamin show are called antioxidants. Found naturally in many foods, these molecules fight "free radicals." When I first heard that term, it sounded like a movement to oppose political prisoners, until I learned that free radicals are toxic oxygen molecules that are released into the body by normal metabolism as well as by stress, smoking, and environmental pollution. Free radicals can attack and do damage to your healthy cells, imposing premature aging and disease on us. So they have *got* to go!

To counterattack, superstars to the rescue! Antioxidants, such as vitamin E, fight back by lowering the risk of heart attack, stroke, high blood pressure, and certain cancers. They do this by preventing the free radicals from messing up the blood vessels in your cardiovascular system. Vitamin E can be found in wheat germ, vegetable oils, and nuts. I put a tablespoon of wheat germ in my health shakes just about every day. But since that kind of habit isn't too common, experts recommend taking a supplement of 100 to 400 IU a day.

That's what my father used to do. He was always taking his vitamin E. The gel caps were his method of choice. We used to tease him about his daily ingestion of what he called "good ol' vitamin E!" For whatever ailed you, he'd say, "You better take some E." You'd have thought it was the magic pill. And maybe it was for him—he lived ninety-three robust years.

Vitamin C is another celebrity compound. Whenever someone has the sniffles these days, the first advice you often hear is, "Pop a vitamin C." Getting your C from orange juice or just plain oranges (which boosts the fiber intake, too) is one way to get it straight from the source.

Ask your doctor if you could benefit from "getting down" with some celebrity compounds.

GET HEALTHY TO A T—WITH TEA

While we're on the subject of antioxidants, you should know that there are certain teas that also contain those immune-system boosters. Some health experts are calling tea the drink for the new millennium. And that's not just because of all the chic tea houses that are popping up across the country, giving the trendy coffee houses competition. It's because of their antioxidant properties.

Black tea, green tea, and oolong are the three types that contain antioxidants. Herbal teas do not. Here's the deal:

The Antioxidant Teas: Black tea is the most popular kind, from the least expensive to the most gourmet. My favorite is English Breakfast. There's also Earl Grey, Irish Breakfast, Darjeeling, and Chinese Keemun.

Green tea, which gets its name from the color of its leaves, is not oxidized. Popular in Japan for centuries, green tea has only recently been recognized in the United States for its health benefits. However, green teas usually contain caffeine, so you may have to look for the decaffeinated brands in specialty tea stores.

Oolong tea is an upscale cross between black and green tea.

The Un-tea: Herbal tea is really a brew of various parts of medicinal botanical plants, rather than real tea leaves. And it doesn't contain the antioxidants that black, green, and oolong have. However, herbal tea serves another purpose by soothing minor maladies. The next time someone at work gets on your last nerve, calm yourself with a cup of chamomile, and you'll see what I mean.

NINE QUICK NUTRITION TRICKS

1. At the grocery store, pick up bags of precut salad fixings.

2. Eat before you go to the mall to avoid chowing down at the food court.

3. Think liquid: Olive and canola oils are better for you than stick butter or solid shortening.

4. Give meat a "supporting cast" role. Most of us even describe our meal by the meat we're having, giving it a starring role: "What's for dinner? Steak." Have you ever described your meal by the *vegetables* you were having? Give stews, soups, casseroles, stir-fry dishes, pastas a chance to take center stage on your menu, and demote the meat. At least let vegetables play catch-up until you can say you give "equal time" to meat and vegetables.

5. Go raw. If the Eddie Murphy movie *Raw* is the closest you have gotten to an uncooked vegetable in the last few years, get yourself a carrot stick—quick!

6. Stop frying for breakfast. Instead of fried eggs, home fries, and bacon, start your day the healthy way—with a low-cook meal full of fruits, grains, juices.

7. Remember the first line of the schoolyard rhyme: Beans, beans, are good for your heart (but don't bother to recite the rest of it).

8. Don't make "all you can eat" a lifestyle.

9. Do something different and adventurous: Visit a health-food store.

AND NOW FOR DESSERT . . . HOW TO CURB THAT SWEET TOOTH

A couple of years ago, a group of African American women participating in a focus group were asked what they thought their worst health habit was. "Eating too many sweets," said one. "I have a sweet tooth that won't quit," replied another.

They are not alone. Each day, American women, in general, add about a ¼ cup of sugar to the foods they eat that may already be sweetened or naturally sweet.

Now, if you are asking, "So what?" here's why that's not good. Too much sugar can:

- Make you gain weight

- Elevate your blood-sugar level

- Make you or your children "hyper" or overactive

- Decay your teeth

To avoid all that, stay healthy, and to maintain a sense of balance, try these strategies:

- *Go natural.* Eat foods that are naturally sweetened, such as fresh fruit (there's that fresh fruit *again!*). At a Japanese restaurant recently, I noticed that orange sections were served for dessert. That hit the sweet spot and none of us had a craving for any other decadent thing.

- *Don't deny yourself the sweet you love.* Allow yourself to have it, say, once a month on a special day (like the day you get your period), rather than whenever whim hits you.

- *Cut back gradually.* I love fudge. There was a time when candy-store displays enticed customers to buy a pound at a time. A quarter pound was the smallest amount you could get—even if all you wanted was a taste. Now, the tide is turning, and I see more two-inch square pieces for sale. I guess when sales began to drop, candymakers started operating on the assumption that a sweet tooth can often be satisfied without being overindulged.

- *Have an alternative.* Bag your own healthy "sweets," such as dried apricots, raisins, or prunes, to have at hand when your craving hits. At restaurants, I have noticed people opting for coffee or tea, rather than a high-calorie, rich dessert. Just remember to refrain from pouring a cup of sugar into your hot drink!

- *Get some harmless "sugar."* Okay, this may be a stretch, but that's no reason not to try it: The next time you feel like having some sugar, go get you a good smooch from your honey. That kind of "sugar" is actually good for you!

THE ULTIMATE—AND THE MOST SIMPLE— NUTRITION TIP OF ALL

Drink lots of water.

That's it. Guzzle as much water each day as you can, and then go back and have some more. Most of us drink water in reaction to thirst, but health experts say that by the time we get thirsty, our bodies are already dehydrated. Have you noticed that increasingly, headlines proclaim that some celebrity has collapsed due to "dehydration"? Don't let that happen to you. Drink at least eight eight-ounce glasses a day, and make that a dozen if you're in an exercise mode.

Besides preventing dehydration, water is especially helpful to fiber, pushing the roughage through your intestines. It also helps your blood flow properly, facilitates digestion, prevents constipation, and reduces your chances of getting kidney stones.

I admit that drinking enough water is my constant challenge—and I've had a few bouts with kidney problems to prove it. But I have found some effective ways to increase my intake. Here are my top five ways:

1. *Take a water bottle with you everywhere you go.* On a trip to Ghana, West Africa, my family and I attended a performance of a comedian who said that he could always spot visiting African Americans—not by the way they walk, talk, or dress—but by those "crazy plastic bottles"! He was referring, of course, to the water bottles tourists carry when we go to foreign countries where we think the tap water may not be safe. But it would be wise to carry them here in the U.S., so that we would drink water more often. I have small water bottles that fit in my purse, and larger bottles for my desk and bedside table. Then there are the middle-size bottles that fit in your car cup-holders. Pick a size that's convenient for you to carry and drink as much water as you can!

2. *Have a glass of water upon rising, and another before you go to bed.* I have a childhood friend who lives in France now. When I went to visit Olivia several years ago, I was pampered not only by her generous hospitality but by the fact that it included a fresh glass of water near the bed that she refreshed each evening in a lovely piece of glassware. It was a personal, caring touch—and I was grateful that having water bedside prevented me from embarrassing myself by tripping over her beautiful furniture in the middle of the night in search of water in the bathroom or kitchen.

3. *When you're out partying, make water your drink of choice.* With a twist of lime or lemon, who'll know the difference?

4. *Drink from every water fountain you pass.* Of course, you don't want to drink from those nasty ones in public places that usually end up spraying you up the nose. But I found working in an office building with fountains in the hallways, every time I had to walk down the hall to the ladies' room, another office, coming or going to work, it

helped to stop and sip. Other places you may frequent with water fountains: schools, colleges, fitness centers, hospitals, department stores, and movie theaters.

5. *Invest in a fancy glass.* You don't have to have a china cabinet full of expensive stemware to buy one special glass from which you enjoy drinking. The one I have is a colorful plastic. In the office, people would often comment, "What a great glass!" Telling folks it was there to help me drink more water was motivation enough for me to actually use it, rather than just have it decorating my desk. And believe me, when you make your goal known to people, they *will* bug you to pursue it. If your goal is to drink more water, they may even come fill your glass when they fill their own.

Exercising Your Options

Either we love to exercise or we hate to. For most of us, there is no in between. But most of us do know that we need it.

Regular, frequent exercise can stave off a whole mess of diseases, illnesses, and conditions. I won't bore you with a list of the things you can get by not keeping your body active, but just keep in mind how much good it would do your body to work out frequently.

THE ULTIMATE EXERCISE TIP

In the previous section, I gave you the 411 on the ultimate in nutrition habits, drinking eight eight-ounce glasses of water a day. Now here's the bomb on the fitness tip: **Exercise three days a week for at least thirty minutes each day.**

If you already do that, good for you! Reward yourself by skipping the next section of this book. But if you need some friendly motivation, like most of us (myself included) do, hang with me. We can do this!

THE EASIEST EXERCISE OF ALL

If you are having a hard time getting regular exercise, try doing it the easy way. Put one foot in front of the other and walk your way to fitness. Exercise experts agree that walking is the best and the easiest way to get and stay fit. It doesn't require special equipment, intense training, or a lot of money. Walking is an equal-opportunity, nondiscriminatory activity.

I can relate to the sedentary lifestyle. From birth, I preferred to sit around than to get up and walk. Believe it or not, I didn't learn to walk until I was twenty-two months old! My father used to tease that I probably thought, *Why should I walk when these fools will carry me?* A diva baby, I didn't even crawl—that would mean messing up my knees! I mainly got around by scooting on my behind. Eventually, however, at nearly two years old, I did get up off my butt, and once I got started, there was no stopping me. By fourth grade, I could outrun everybody in my class—boys included. By high school graduation, I was voted "Most Soulful Strut" (whatever that meant!). As a young adult in New York City, I saved a lot of subway and taxi fares, because frankly, I preferred to walk. These days, I hit my neighborhood park during warm weather, and my treadmill at home in the winter. I admit I'm not *always* motivated for workout walking, but once I get with it, it feels good to be doing something I know is beneficial for my body. So during the course of my life, I went from scooting around the floor on my behind to power-walking around the track in my DKNYs. If I can do that, you can surely get up from the couch. You're already halfway there! (And believe me, shopping for those walking shoes is a motivational first step.)

By doing what comes naturally—walking that walk—all of us can reap a multitude of health benefits. Did you know:

- That fitness walking can take off fat and reduce stress, and stave off a whole lot of other ills?

- That a brisk walk for a little as half an hour a day may keep a heart attack away?

- That walking regularly keeps you "regular"?

- That brisk walking, or other exercise, done three times a week for at least twenty minutes may reduce the pressure within the eye that leads to glaucoma?

- That walking not only tones your legs but also can take off fat anywhere—from arms to thighs?

- That a study of mostly black women in Florida with stressful jobs showed they had a 30 percent reduction in work stress after eight weeks of fitness walking?

Remember walking to school (that is, unless you were bused) when you were a kid? Well, if you haven't done the stroll since then, get on up! It's an exercise that can last a lifetime. Free your legs, and your mind will follow!

It's as simple as that, but just in case you'd like more details on how to walk for maximum efficiency, here are some basics for shaping your program:

Start out slowly. For the beginner, the word is take it *slow.* If you've never exercised regularly, or haven't done it in a long time, try just five minutes at first. Walk around your block, or to the grocery store, or the mailbox.

Step on up. Increase your commitment by walking for a longer period of time. Try out a track at a high school or local park (pay *no* attention to all those jocks racing around you.) Work up to a half hour three times a week.

Choose a comfortable pace. You should never feel tired or sore after your walk—nor should you be gasping for breath.

Don't go too far. Don't get so carried away that you're too tired to walk back. Gradually you will get to know your limits.

Set a goal, and stick to it. Eventually work yourself up to walking three times a week for thirty to forty-five minutes. To lose weight, especially if it's only ten pounds, you'll want to walk at least five days a week, the longer the better. It all depends on your needs and lifestyle. If you walk a fifteen- to twenty-minute-mile pace, you can probably walk an hour every day without harm. If you love speedwalking, then you may need to take days off. You can walk fast one day, rest or stroll the next.

Don't pump your arms. This is a misunderstanding of the racewalking technique. The power of the body is in the legs, and hips, not the shoulders and arms. Pumping will only make your shoulders tense and tired.

Do keep the body aligned. Think about the racewalkers you've seen who walk fast but don't lean forward. Leaning will create a strain on your back. Walk tall!

BEYOND WALKING

The key to staying motivated is to find an activity that you enjoy doing. If you like to swim, for example, you won't mind doing it several times a week. If you're known to boogie on down, dancerobics, jazzercise, or African dance class might keep you dedicated. Plus, if you pick a sport or fitness activity that suits your personality, you are more likely to stick with it. There are really only two reasons to indulge in fitness anyway: for health benefits and for fun. The second reason is what more of us need to focus on. Once you've found a workout that you think is fun, and fits your schedule and your budget, all you've got to do is do it—and reap the benefits of a healthy lifestyle.

KNOW YOUR GOAL

Go for the goal—but first set one by figuring out just what are you exercising for. Are you working out to lose weight, to increase cardiovascular endurance, to firm up and tone your body, or simply to reduce stress?

If **weight loss** is your goal, these activities burn a lot of calories and are good choices:

- Aerobics

- In-line skating

- Running

- Rowing

- Speed walking

For **cardiovascular benefits,** try:

- Cycling

- Running

- Skiing

- Step training

- Swimming

- Walking

For **toning and shaping** your body, try strength training, or picking two or three sports that you enjoy. Alternating activities that work out the upper parts of your body one day, and the lower body another day can give you a total body workout.

To **reduce stress,** choose an exercise that takes you away from your source of tension. If you get stressed inside your home or in an office, get outside. If you have a dog, take it for a walk in the park or the woods. If your origin of stress comes from the outside world (if you work with the public, for example), seek peace with a solitary step routine or weightlifting.

USE YOUR ASSETS TO YOUR ADVANTAGE

1. If you are **tall,** you have the advantage in volleyball and basketball.

2. Others may call it fat, but you know that **extra body fat** can contribute to buoyancy in the water that gives you an edge in swimming, water aerobics, scuba diving, and snorkeling.

3. **Long arms** make it easier for you to play racquet sports, aerobic boxing, and volleyball.

4. **Large thighs** mean strong thighs for skating (in-line, roller, or ice), hiking, cycling, skiing, rock climbing.

5. If you have a **large body frame,** you're more likely to withstand the stress and strain of contact sports, such as hockey, soccer, and basketball. You can also do well in softball and weight training.

6. **The smaller the body frame,** the more likely you are to enjoy kayaking, diving, and gymnastics.

7. **Flexible,** are you? Try figure-skating, tai chi, fencing, or kickboxing.

8. Being **lean and mean** gives you more energy and stamina for strenuous sports like marathon running, gymnastics, and rock climbing.

9. Think Dominique Dawes. **Short legs** give you a lower center of gravity that translates into greater balance for gymnastics, fencing, squash, racquetball, downhill skiing.

10. **Long legs** mean you have a longer stride that's an advantage in basketball, swimming, distance running, cross-country skiing.

11. If you have **broad shoulders,** you lend power to your arms that give you the potential to be a powerful swimmer, tennis player, volleyball player, rower, or softball player.

12. **Upper-body strength** makes you suited for: golf, aerobic boxing, swimming.

Notice that basketball, swimming, and gymnastics were named most often, so they cut across body types. If you don't see yourself on the list above, don't despair—just pick a sport that *you* will enjoy! Again, the key to fulfilling your mission in fitness—or anything else, for that matter—is to do what gives you joy.

CAN WE TALK—ABOUT SISTERS AND SWIMMING?

Swimming may be high on the list of sports that are suited to most body types, but it definitely hasn't always been high on the popularity list for African American women. I know from personal experience.

When I was in college, my predominately black school required that students pass swimming in order to graduate. This caused much anxiety among the women students because of the many psychological hang-ups African American women have had concerning getting our hair wet after it's gone through the extensive and expensive process of straightening. And even though many of us had converted to "naturals," we still carried the fear—even when it was moot. In addition, there were a few overweight students who assumed that swimming would be as difficult and embarrassing an endeavor as gymnastics.

As it came closer to the prescribed time to take the swimming course, people did all sorts of shameless and astonishing things to get out of it. For example, some came up with letters from their parents saying they saw no reason why this class should be required if one was, say, a drama major. And believe me, the antics people pulled to get out of swimming class—such as seeing the school psychologist—produced much drama.

I could relate to a certain degree. Afraid of water myself, I had flunked the Guppies class at the YWCA when I was eleven. But failing classes in college wasn't part of my plan—I wanted to graduate magna cum laude. So I worked on submerging my anxiety and became determined to take the swimming class and pass it without drowning my dignity.

When the dreaded day arrived in my sophomore year, I felt it was just my luck to get the professor who had the worst reputation for having absolutely no sympathy. However, on our first day, Ms. No-Nonsense informed my Swimming 101 class that there was nothing to be afraid of, and that indeed, the students who would emerge from her class as the best swimmers—the ones who would get the A's—would be the biggest girls.

"Those of you who have the most meat on your bones stand to be the best swimmers," she said forthrightly. "That's because you are the most buoyant."

Not trusting her, we looked on in trepidation as she singled out the full-figured sister who had exhibited the most fear. "You," she said, pointing to this poor girl. "You follow my direction and show everyone how to float." The student reluctantly did as she was told—and sure enough, she stayed on top of the water far easier than any of the rest of us. By the end of the semester, that student could not only swim better than anyone in the class, but her self-confidence was sky high and it showed. Her backstroke was something to see!

No matter what your body type—or hair type, for that matter—swimming is hard to beat as an aerobic exercise. Unlike other fitness activities such as cycling, running, and rowing, swimming uses nearly all the major muscle groups. It places an effective demand on the heart and lungs and also improves posture and flexibility. A refreshing change of pace from other fitness regimens, putting in a half hour of laps three times a week is a good outlet for tension and stress. Plus, swimming can give you a psychological feeling of enjoyment and accomplishment that's called a "swimmer's high." That's what boosted the self-esteem of the big girl in my college class, who got a good grade. I got a C in the class. At least I had passed. Halleluia!

Even if you don't know how to swim, you can benefit from water fitness classes called "aquarobics," "aquacise," "aqua tone," and "water aerobics," to name a few. These classes are excuse-proof for the hair-obsessed and contact-lens wearers like me because you never have to put your head under water.

Most important, the pushing, pulling, and kicking against the water provide up to forty times the resistance that air does, so water workouts burn more calories than dry-land exercise that are done in the same time interval. Plus, it's a stress reliever because, just like taking a bath, becoming one with water makes us feel tranquil and relaxed. If you dislike working out alone, water aerobics can be enjoyed with others—young or old, skinny or obese, healthy or arthritic, nonswimmers or jocks. Look for the classes at your local YWCA, gyms and fitness clubs that have pools, and vacation resorts. I've tried water aerobics classes myself, and felt that at last there was a water activity (besides going on a cruise) that I could actually not just endure, but enjoy.

When it comes to swimming, with the many choices and freedoms to wear our hair slicked back, close cropped, Nubian twisted, or dreadlocked, there should be fewer inhibitions than there used to be. In fact, I know the hip-hop generation is freer than previous generations were, thank goodness. My four girls all swim like fish.

STILL NOT PERSUADED TO EXERCISE?

If finding the sport for your body type hasn't moved you off the couch, then I have two more suggestions.

First, pick a sport based on your personality type.

> *If you are the social type,* you may prefer fitness classes, team sports, and one-on-one games.
>
> *If you like to be alone,* walking, running, cycling, skating, swimming, skiing, and weight training are solitary pursuits.
>
> *Always challenging yourself or looking for an adventure?* Try rock climbing or training for a marathon.
>
> *If you're the competitive type,* tennis, volleyball, soccer, and other team sports may appeal to you.
>
> *Are you a busybody?* Fast-paced activities, such as African dance, step-aerobics, low-impact aerobics, squash, or racquetball will keep you on the move.

Second, if all else fails, do what comes naturally, like housework. Each of the following activities burns 150 calories.

> **Mowing your lawn,** 18 minutes
>
> **Walking your dog,** 30 minutes
>
> **Pushing the cart at the grocery store,** 30 minutes

Weeding your yard, 34 minutes

Washing your car yourself, 35 minutes

Vacuuming, 38 minutes

Washing windows, 40 minutes

Playing the piano, 40 minutes

Raking leaves, 44 minutes

NO TIME TO EXERCISE?

You've got a time-consuming job. You're a club woman, doing great things for the community. You're a churchwoman, giving your all for religious causes. You have children to rear, your spouse needs some attention. And oh, the Internet beckons. It's the biggest hindrance to physical activity: no time.

The truth is that we never *get* enough time—we have to *make* time. Sometimes, to do that, we have to multitask, or combine our duties. Grab your time to exercise by combining it with other things. For example, you can:

Take Baby to the gym. Don't let having an infant or toddler keep you from getting back into shape after childbirth. Many fitness clubs, gyms, and YWCAs have Mommy-Baby classes or child care that allows you to exercise in peace.

Work out with your children. Take swimming lessons when you take the kids for theirs. Let them teach you how to in-line skate. Take a dance class at your daughter's ballet school. Target a weekend for a family bike trip—even if it's just around the neighborhood.

Exercise with your honey. Go for walks together. Join the same gym. If you both work out at home, put your treadmill next to his bench press. Learn a new sport together, like skiing or tennis. Try a different type of vacation, such as a hiking trip or a spa cruise.

Catch up on other things as you work out. Read a magazine on the treadmill. Listen to an audiobook while you power walk. Play golf with a colleague.

Start an exercise class at church. Gospel aerobics, anyone? Amen!

🗝 *Healthy Habits* 🗝

If life is a journey, here's a road map. Get in the habit of making these stops along the road to good health:

Go to the Doctor When You Are Well

It's called prevention. Getting medical, dental, and eye appointments at regular intervals suggested by your health-care providers establishes a baseline on which you can judge illness. For example, you have to know what a mammogram of your breast looks like when it's healthy in order to recognize a problem. Your healthy breast doesn't look like anyone else's. Getting an accurate picture of your own unique breast is called a "baseline mammography."

If you've ever had a baby, you know you were asked to take the child to the pediatrician for "well baby" appointments so the doctor could track his or her first months. Well, you need "well adult" appointments, too. Here are some you need to make—and keep—to maintain good health:

Physical exam: From ages eighteen to thirty-nine, get a physical every three years. At age forty and over, once a year. This exam should reveal any abnormal or recurring ailments.

Dental appointment: Dentists recommend that you get your beautiful smile checked every six months; once a year, at the very least. Pain, swelling, or other abnormalities require immediate attention.

Eye exam: Eye doctors want to see you at least every two years, to check for glaucoma or to see if you need glasses or a lens-prescription change.

Other appointments to keep:

Mammogram: Because black women tend to develop breast cancer earlier than American women of other races, it is recommended that starting at age thirty-five we go for our baseline mammogram (the first one that subsequent mammograms are compared to). Other women should have their first mammogram at age forty. Then until age forty-nine, all of us should go every one to two years. Ages fifty and over, once a year.

Clinical breast exam: To detect cancer or a precancerous mass in the breast, have your breasts checked once a year. This is usually part of a complete gyn exam. In addition, be sure to learn how to perform a breast self-examination. It is vital that you do this once a month.

Pelvic exam with Pap smear: Sexually active teens and every woman by the age of eighteen should have this test by a gynecologist once a year. Postmenopausal women can be tested every three years (unless you're at high risk for developing cervical cancer, which would necessitate continuing a yearly exam schedule).

Blood cholesterol test: Every five years, if first test is normal; as recommended by your doctor if level is elevated.

Rectal exam: Once a year for folks over forty, to check for colorectal cancer.

Fecal occult blood test: A stool smear to detect the presence of blood; a screening test for cancer of the colon and rectum, it should be taken once a year after age forty.

BE IN CONTROL OF YOUR REPRODUCTIVE HEALTH

Growing up, or I should say "trying to get grown," is hard enough without the complications that sexuality brings. From the onset of adolescence, contracting a sexually transmitted disease (STD) can interfere with your ability to feel self-confident and trusting of others. At worst, an STD can result in infertility and lifelong illness. An unplanned pregnancy can throw the best-laid plans and hopes into a tailspin.

Taking control of your reproductive health is not just a sexuality issue; it has ramifications that can affect your potential and capacity for achievement. When you don't feel in control, it's almost impossible to excel at pursuing your sexual purpose. Your sexuality should have a purpose beyond instant pleasure. In order to achieve whatever that purpose is (i.e., healthy loving, planned parenthood, STD/HIV prevention), you need to have full control of your own sexual health.

In the office of my ob-gyn, I found the following important information about taking control of women's health that I would like to share with you, reprinted with permission of the Organon Pharmaceutical Company:

Adolescents

Sexually Transmitted Diseases (STDs)—AIDS, chlamydia, herpes, gonorrhea, syphilis: *The issues:* STDs are easy to catch and easy to spread—through sex. They can have life effects for the rest of your life; can be fatal; can be avoided.

> *STDs can always be avoided by:* Not having sex, "abstinence."
> *STDs can often—but not always—be avoided by:*

- Knowing as much as you can about your partner.

- Always having condoms with you if you think you might have sex.

- Always insisting that your partner use condoms.

- Knowing how to talk to your partner about your needs and values.

- If you even think you may have been exposed to an STD, see a doctor as soon as possible.

Birth Control

You can get pregnant at any time after you have had your first period, at any time of the month—there's no such thing as a "safe time."

- You can get pregnant *any*time you have sex.

- You are the only one who can control whether you get pregnant or not.

- Be aware of the pressure you may get from your partner and friends and decide in advance how you want to respond.

- Know how to talk to your partner about your needs and values.

Birth control is available at any age: If you are sexually active, inform yourself about contraceptives. You can choose the Pill, condoms, foam, a diaphragm, the Sponge, or abstinence.

Sexual Abuse

At any age, the decision to have sex is yours alone:

- If you are threatened, that's *wrong.*

- If you are forced by anyone, including family members, that's a crime.

If you have been forced or threatened:

- You have legal rights.

- Nothing will happen to you if you discuss it with the proper authorities or a therapist. If you think you might be pregnant or have been hurt, see a doctor right away.

Sexually Mature Women

Birth Control

There are options at any age:

- Forty used to be considered too old to have children—that's changed.

- Forty used to be thought of as too old to take the Pill—that has changed for healthy nonsmoking women.

Your choices: The Pill, IUDs, foam, condoms, diaphragm, the Sponge, tubal ligation; a partner's vasectomy; abstinence.

- Look into the advantages and disadvantages of each method.

- Investigate the Pill's responsibility for causing cardiovascular disease, breast disease, uterine problems, and osteoporosis (loss of bone density).

- Discuss with your doctor disadvantages of the Pill in relation to breakthrough bleeding, other birth control methods, and continuing a pregnancy conceived while on the Pill.

Regular Checkups for You and Your Partner

Many diseases are preventable by regular checkups: Men and women need regular checkups. Men sometimes need to be prodded; use your checkup as an opportunity to remind your partner to be checked. There's a lot of variety to what's "normal." *Your choices:* The best prevention for breast cancer is monthly breast self-exam, regular checkups, and mammograms. Ask about unusual symptoms, such as discharge from nipples, lumps, dimpling of skin. Regular checkups can detect cervical cancer in its earliest stage. Tell your doctor if you are experiencing irregular bleeding—most is

okay. The Pap smear was developed to detect cervical cancer.
Tell your doctor if you bleed for a long time or have frequent
periods.

MENOPAUSAL YEARS

Menopause: What is it and when do I know if it's time?

> *Menopause is a normal part of the reproductive cycle:* You *can*
> understand it. You can make choices about how to deal with it.
> You can make choices about how to manage it. You may get
> understanding and support from your partner.

> *Menopausal symptoms—What are they, who has them, how long
> do they last?* Ask your doctor what can be done about hot
> flashes. Ask about what can be done about vaginal dryness,
> painful sex, and reduced interest in sex. Ask about help for
> moodiness, anxiety, depression, insomnia.

Hormone-Replacement Therapy (HRT)

> *There are advantages and disadvantages to different therapies:*
> Become familiar with the differences between HRT and the
> Pill. HRT isn't for everyone.

> *Who can undergo HRT and who can't:* Ask your doctor about
> treatment options if you've had a hysterectomy. HRT offers
> prevention against osteoporosis. HRT offers prevention
> against cardiovascular disease. HRT can help with your
> quality of life. Discuss your concerns about breast and uterine
> disease. Ask what tests you need to have. Ask what you can
> expect after you start therapy.

KNOW YOUR FAMILY HEALTH HISTORY

Finding out the diseases and conditions that plagued your parents,
grandparents, and siblings can give you an idea of what you may be at
high risk for developing. Cancers, diabetes, kidney disease, sickle cell

anemia, and other conditions can run in families for generations. Knowing the conditions you have a propensity for can help you and your doctor make lifestyle changes or take medical intervention.

Ask family members about illnesses throughout their lives, and get information on the cause of death of deceased relatives to create your own family health tree. There is computer software for this, and some computers, such as the iMac, offer a medical history template.

Armed with this information, you will know what conditions to research, and what symptoms to be on the lookout for. Observing the medical care of relatives can also get you a foundation for what healthy habits you need to develop yourself. It's a first step in taking control of your health.

PLAY THE NUMBERS

Quick: How old are you? What's your birthdate? What's your Social Security number? Your telephone number? Your address? Your ATM code? The number of boyfriends you had in high school?

These are numbers that you can probably rattle off the top of your head. But how well do you know your blood pressure? Your cholesterol level? Your body mass index (BMI)? These are important numbers too. You may not need to recite them to impress anyone, and you may not need to repeat them as often as you do your phone, fax, or cell numbers, but you should know them enough to know if they are high or low, healthy or dangerous, so you can do something about them if they don't make the grade. So let's start with the blood pressure.

KEEP THE PRESSURE OFF

When people say, "I've got to watch my pressure," what do they mean? High blood pressure is indicated when the pressure of the blood pumped from the heart through the arteries is elevated, making the heart work harder. When the heart doesn't have to work very hard, it's low to normal. We do need it to work, of course, but too much pressure for too long can lead to stroke or heart attack. It's determined by two numbers, the *systolic,* the pressure exerted when the heart beats, over the *diastolic,* when the heart is at rest between beats. Normal is 135/85 or lower. Borderline is 135/85 to 140/90. High is 140/90 or above. If your pressure is over 145/95, you are considered *hypertensive*. The numbers to hit: 120/80. As you probably know, you get this test when you go to the doctor and the nurse puts that black Velcro strap around your arm and pumps it up.

What can I do about high blood pressure? What causes high blood pressure is not known, but here's what you should know:

- African Americans are at high risk

- Your risk is doubled if hypertension runs in your family

- If you are overweight, don't get enough exercise, or have a lot of stress, you are at risk

With healthy lifestyle changes and if your doctor prescribes drugs, high blood pressure can be treated. To help prevent it:

- Have your pressure checked as often as your physician advises

- Shake off the salt. Eat no more than 2,000 milligrams of salt a day—that's just less than one teaspoon. (See more information on salt-busting later in this chapter.)

- Shake it up, baby: Increase your exercise frequency

- Practice stress reduction. (See Chapter Three, "Relax, Refresh, and Revive.")

- Don't smoke.

KNOW THE DOWN-LOW ON CHOLESTEROL

What is high cholesterol, anyway? Elevated blood cholesterol produces plaque-filled fatty deposits in the arteries, impeding blood flow. If left uncontrolled, this can lead to heart disease.

Cholesterol travels through the body by lipoproteins. There are two types of lipoproteins; high-density lipoproteins (HDLs, the "good" cholesterol) and low-density lipoproteins (LDLs, the "bad" cholesterol). The total of both are measured, along with the ratio between the total and the HDL. The number that's a winner is less than 200 total cholesterol. A healthy ratio is below 4. Your doctor can advise you on how to conduct this test.

What can I do about high cholesterol? You can help tip your ratio in the right direction with a lifestyle of eating low in fat and lots of exercise. If your cholesterol is too high, your doctor may prescribe a medication.

Keep an Eye on Your BMI

What's body mass index? BMI is a measure of fitness that determines weight in relation to height. You can figure this one out yourself—just get out your calculator: Divide your weight in pounds by the square of your height in inches and multiply that number by 705. For example, at 5 feet 5 (or 65 inches) and 115 pounds, I calculate my BMI like this: 65 times 65 equals 4,225; divide 115 by the 4,225; then multiply that 0.0272189 by 705 to equal 19.18. The target number is below 27.

What can I do about it? Women with a number calculation of 19 or less have the lowest death rates. However, you can be overweight without being obese. If you're firm, you're probably fine. But if you're flabby, lower your BMI with aerobic exercise, a low-fat diet, and strength training to firm up those muscles.

Please, Don't Smoke

This message is so pervasive that it's a real mystery to me why anyone would still be smoking. But I am told that once one starts, it's so addictive it just isn't easy to stop. Plus, one has to have the desire to quit—and people who smoke enjoy smoking.

Since millions of people are lighting up today, the reasons why that's not a great idea bear repeating: It causes cancer and aggravates many other diseases to start sooner—and sometimes kill quicker. Just because it's legal doesn't mean it's not lethal. Smoking related diseases can be prevented.

If you smoke, please try to stop. We need you—and we need you healthy and here. Your local chapter of the American Cancer Society can help.

If you don't smoke, don't start. And help to spread that message to our youth.

I'm sure you can think of even more everyday ways to stay safe and well. Most healthy habits are just common sense put into common practice. When they do become habits, they become the basis for your healthy lifestyle. That's what it's really all about. To fulfill your ultimacy, to be your best, the mission doesn't have to be about being a jock, saying you're a vegetarian, or even working out day in and day out. It's all about being in the habit of living a healthy life.

💜 *Your Optimum Health Journal** 💜

What are your seven most healthful habits?

What unhealthy habits would you like to change?

Your blood pressure:

Your cholesterol level:

Your BMI:

List one way to improve any of the above that are not at optimum level:

List exercise that I know I can do three days a week for thirty minutes:

My favorite healthy foods:

*If you don't wish to write in this book, make a photocopy of this page, or write in your own journal.

Create your personal "Good Health" contract and sign it below.

Signed: _____ *Date:* _____

$\mathcal{S}$PIRITUALITY

The source of purpose is spirituality. That is, a belief in a higher power that gives life meaning. Without spirituality, you may be able to obtain fame, you may be able to gain great wealth. But you cannot gain great*ness* and your utmost purpose in life without acknowledging that it comes from an utmost place. Your purpose is larger than you; it is for a greater good, and the creative source from which it comes is higher than you. It is necessary to know that the force that manifests your purpose within you is infinitely greater in magnitude than your earthly mind and body.

♥ *Your Spiritual Style* ♥

Once you know that higher power, you can rely on it—and relying on that knowledge is what spirituality is all about. Through a combination of divine guidance and human effort, you can reach your highest purpose. How you approach your purpose can be called your "spiritual style."

Here are a few quick questions to ask yourself to determine your style.

1. Do you define your spiritual quest as:

A. Finding a connection to God

B. Fulfilling an emotional need

C. Leading a good and moral life

D. Finding inner peace

2. Do you seek spirituality:

A. As a member of a religious group or congregation

B. By following a religious leader

C. By nurturing and serving others

D. Mainly by yourself

3. Your primary tools for spirituality are:

A. Worship service

B. Self-help books and tapes

C. Interaction with people and nature

D. Prayer and meditation

If you answered mostly A's, you are probably more religious than spiritual. If your answers were mainly B's, you're a follower whose faith helps overcome struggles and obstacles. Answers with two or three C's means you use spirituality for guidance in morality. D answers indicate a quest for the inner peace that solitude provides. Of course, it's possible to have a mix of them all. In that case, you have an eclectic spiritual style—you're free-spirited. And that's alright, too.

💚 *Take Yourself Higher* 💚

When you are open to a larger knowing, the messages that will come to take you higher won't surprise you. We recognize that sense of knowing in others, yet we are slower to acknowledge it in ourselves.

Take Dana Christmas, for example. People who know her were not surprised to hear that she demonstrated heroism in a horrible dormitory fire that killed three students and injured fifty-eight others at Seton Hall University in South Orange, New Jersey, in January 2000.

According to an account by Meg Nugent in the *Newark Star-Ledger* newspaper, the twenty-one-year-old resident assistant "could have rushed out into the frigid night, clearing the poison from her lungs, sparing her body the horrors of burning." Instead, she "raced from room to room on the freshman dormitory's third floor, pounding on doors, screaming for students to wake up, to get out, even as she gulped in the incapacitating fumes that slowed her escape and allowed the flames to reach her."

Something great within Dana Christmas emerged that day. And that higher force saved the lives of several students, as well as her own. By all accounts, Dana, a criminal justice major and aspiring lawyer who is recovering from burns over 60 percent of her body and painful skin graft operations, had long been on the path to greatness. "She seemed older than she was. She was always interested in people and how they felt," said David Kott, her high school history teacher. "She was always wanting to help people all the time."

Dana's responsibility as a resident assistant was to aid and supervise the college students that lived in her residence hall. But her heroism was in something she did far beyond her job description: She cared. And that kind of action comes from the spirit.

Her story proves that it's not necessarily your job, or what you *do* that manifests your ultimate self. It's who you *are,* it's what's inside, it's your spiritual light that shines through every action and every breath you take. Your purpose may be made plain in the subtle habit of wanting to help people all the time, as well as in the heroics of the heat of a fire. It all comes from the same source of spiritual power.

As you grow spiritually, you will have a greater understanding of your purpose. Yet you don't have to be a silver senior to obtain that wisdom. Dana, at twenty-one, had spiritual maturity that gave others the impression that she was older than her chronological age. Growing spiritually and growing old are not necessarily the same thing—although for many people the two do coincide. But for the most part, it's not an age thing. It's a spirit thing.

Being a nice person doesn't always mean that you are using your spirit to its best advantage, either. Michelle Burford, who is also in her twenties, says she used to be "a pleaser." Here is her story of growing up in Phoenix, as one of ten children:

"I turned myself inside out to please my parents," she tells me. "I knew they loved me, but deep down, I thought I could make them love me *more* by being the golden child—the one who never 'talked back,' the one who made perfect grades, and most of all, the one my mother could depend on to grow up and make her proudest. I thought that being the nice girl—and rarely speaking up with my opinions or daring to show a side of my personality that my mother wouldn't like—was a way for me to capture her approval, her gold star.

"In college, my first major was nursing. But looking back, even that choice was based on what I thought my parents expected, which was that I choose a major that would lead to a more concrete career path than writing—a dream I'd always had. Though my parents never pressured me to choose medicine, I heaped what I imagined their expectations to be on my own back.

"One night, my best friend at college and I sat complaining about hating the nursing program, when she said something that changed everything. 'Michelle, will your parents be there when you're fifty, changing bedpans and totally hating your life?' At that moment, I made a choice to let go of the burden of trying to please every one else—which always left *me* the most unhappy.

"The next semester, I changed my major to English with an emphasis in journalism. At first my parents gave me a few raised eyebrows—'What are you going to do with an *English* degree?' Now even they see the value in me following my passion, because it has turned into a life's work that they know I care about.

"The irony is that all along, it was really me—not my parents—who chose to have a crazy idea of what my career was supposed to be, or what I was supposed to be. In a sense, getting over 'the disease to please' meant wrestling with the voices in my own head."

After college graduation, Michelle moved to Colorado Springs, Colorado, to work for a group of magazines, where she was one of only a few Black people in town. There, away from familial expectations, she excelled in her work and was quickly promoted. That competence and confidence gave her the courage to apply for a job at a national magazine, *Essence,* in New York. Her talent was recognized there as well, and in less than a year, she was promoted to senior editor. Word got around of her rising star, and when the founding editor of *O, The Oprah Magazine* began looking to staff that publication, Michelle was one of the first to be hired, as senior features editor. And after just six months there, she was promoted to deputy editor. She has since left to pursue a freelance editing and writing career, while continuing to contribute to *O.* Stepping out of the comfort zone of pleasing others to please her own spirit allowed her to find a new zone of comfort: following her own mission.

In her job, Michelle worked closely with Oprah Winfrey, who stated in the first issue of her magazine that she, too, used to have the "disease to please." Like Michelle, she would do what others asked of her—even if it inconvenienced her—so that people would have a favorable impression of her and like her. Coincidentally, on her TV show, I heard Oprah's guest Gary Zukav, author of the bestselling *The Seat of the Soul,* advise that in such situations people should "share who you are and what you need in a considerate way. If you try to please by doing what others want because you think they'll get mad, you do not honor them or you."

That is one of the major elements of spirituality: Honor. Showing utmost respect for someone you hold in high esteem is the manifestation of honor. Just as we honor God, and honor others, and we must also honor ourselves. In so doing, we remain true to our spirit.

Here are some other elements of spirituality:

BELIEF

Saint Augustine said, "For what is faith unless it is to believe what you do not see?"

Think about it: There are many things that we do not *know* are true, yet we *believe* that they are. How do we know air exists? We have committed our intellect to an idea or judgment that has been taught to us or that we learned. We believe in things unseen. Belief in God is the ultimate faith.

As a child, one of the first songs I learned to sing in the junior church choir and play on the piano was called "I Believe." I still have the original sheet music to the song that ends with these words:

> I BELIEVE *above the storm the smallest pray'r will still be heard.*
> I BELIEVE *that someone in the great somewhere hears ev'ry word.*
> *Ev'ry time I hear a newborn baby cry, or touch a leaf, or see the sky,*
> *Then I know why I BELIEVE!*

Notice that the songwriters put the words I BELIEVE in capital letters. The song also says that the *smallest* prayer will still be heard. As a small girl, I translated that to mean my own little prayers. So at a young age I came to feel that beliefs were important. As a result, I also learned that depending on one's beliefs is a spiritual *action*. Believing isn't a passive act. In fact, to believe one must take positive and powerful action. Believing in ourselves helps us to expect that we can achieve the things we need. Believing in God helps us to know that we are aided in those things we need to do. Just when you think you can't do anything more, your beliefs can carry you through. Believing guides us through uncertainty. In a time of adversity, instead of giving up you might be prone to think: *In God, all things are possible.* And when that thought becomes a belief, it fortifies your soul.

Believing is the hallmark secret of our "soul purpose." It allows us to commit our minds and our souls to unseen powers that can turn a difficult situation into an easier path. It can make those people with blind minds see the light. Belief can turn you from down-and-out into up-and-at-'em. Belief can make the difference between success and failure.

In 1997, I was fortunate enough to go to Robben Island in South Africa, the place of banishment and brutality off the coast of beautiful Cape Town where Nelson Mandela was imprisoned for twenty-seven years. "Here," our tour guide said, pointing out an old quarry, "in this mine is where our president toiled just about everyday of his imprisonment." He explained the harsh conditions, including the constant exposure to the fine grit that can seep into one's eyes and cause sight problems. The hard labor of breaking big rocks into little ones could take a physical toll. And looking over at Cape Town's lovely skyline strikingly defined by Table Mountain, I thought that being so near, yet so far, from freedom must have been excruciating.

Fortunately for our brothers and sisters in South Africa, and for the world, Nelson Mandela and the other freedom fighters who spent so many years on Robben Island, could not be stripped of their beliefs. Holding on to the belief that one day they would be free, the comrades continued over the years to discuss the struggle against apartheid, and to strategize about what they would do once they were released from prison. Naysayers could have told them that they did these things in vain. Most people looking at the situation as it was, could have been tempted to dissuade a prisoner working in a quarry from thinking that one day he would be free—much less president of the country. But Mandela not only kept up his physicality by performing the hard labor, he held on to his belief of freedom and majority rule. In so doing, he became president. The prison where Mandela toiled for many years is now a museum dedicated to the power of the transformation of the human spirit. Amazing grace!

Such examples of the lowest becoming the highest can give us reasons to hold on to our own beliefs. When an athlete believes that she can make it to the finish line, when an accident victim believes that he will walk again, when a mother believes that a wayward child will return to the right path—all these are the first steps in the journey to making something extraordinary happen.

It has been said so many times that it is almost cliché, but it still bears repeating because it is true: What we conceive, we can achieve, if we only believe.

Start believing. If you believe in God, you can learn to believe in yourself. If you believe in yourself, you can certainly believe in the power of the Most High.

FAITH

Belief is truth held in the mind. Faith is a fire in the heart.

— JOSEPH FORT NEWTON

Faith addresses a system of allegiances that can define your spirituality. Another church song I know asks, "Where is your faith in God?"

Do you know where yours is? Is it somewhere placed up high that's hard to reach? Is it somewhere on a shelf that's inaccessible? Is it hidden in a closet? If so, it's time to "out" it! Get your faith out of the closet. Tell it to come on out in the open where it can breathe free. Have the courage to follow your faith in God, and in life, and in yourself. Get on out with it!

An acquaintance of mine, Caryl Lucas, e-mailed me in 1999 to say that she was leaving her reporting job at a large urban newspaper after a distinguished tenure to pursue freelance fashion writing:

> Thursday is my last day at the newspaper. I'm moving on and stepping out on faith after 16 years. It's time to grow, and let go, and take the less familiar road. I'm so excited, as well as anxious, but I'm prayerfully asking God to lead me in all decisions and be my guide. It's amazing, the support and the blessings I'm receiving thus far, be it leads or just love, coming my way as I explore all options and open myself on all levels—spiritually, professionally and emotionally. I've always admired your fortitude and ability to sew into the lives of women, especially sister-friends, and your many colleagues. . . . If you have any words of wisdom or advice to offer, I welcome your input.

It happened that just that morning I was cleaning out files in my electronic notebook and came across one I had titled "Backup Plan." Not recalling which of my many schemes that was, I opened it. Inside, looking at the date and the notes, I realized that I had jotted down some potential ways to make a living in case I were to lose my job. When I made this list, I had just heard that the magazine on which I worked might be sold to another publishing company in a different city. Weighing my options, I had jotted down sources of income I could pursue, such as a book deal, freelance writing, speaking engagements, ideas for an editorial consulting business. I would need those notes because the magazine was moved from New York City to Washington, D.C., and I decided to follow my plan instead of the magazine's plan. I eventually did all those things—and everything turned out just fine. Scrolling down to the end of the note, I found the secret to the successful outcome. These words were in boldface: **GOD WILL TAKE CARE OF YOU. KEEP THE FAITH.**

Two years after affirming the faith I believed would carry me through, I felt blessed to be able to type these words of gratitude and closure: . . . AND HE/SHE HAS! THANK YOU, GOD! YOU ARE SO GOOD.

In my e-mail reply to my friend, I related that story, hoping that it might give her the courage to step out more boldly on the faith that was leading her. As I knew she would, Caryl landed firmly on her feet. She's loving her new work as a freelance fashion writer.

Martin Luther King, Jr., said, "Take the first step in faith. You don't have to see the whole staircase, just take the first step."

When you step out on faith, you are walking in the right direction. Keep on stepping and you'll reach your ultimate purpose.

Shortly after my journalism colleague stepped out on faith, another friend, who lives in Europe, sent me an e-mail saying that his mother, who lives in New York, had recently revealed that she had a spot of cancer on her colon. In asking his good friends to form a cyber circle of prayer, I was especially moved by how he signed off on the message, "Faith Without Fear." He was making it clear that the fear he could have been feeling if he allowed himself was definitely in check by his faith in a positive outcome. That gave his friends—like me—who should have been cheering him up, the courage to respond in an affectionate and supportive way. His faith inspired us to live our own lives similarly, in faith without fear.

Faith, like Purpose (*Nia*), is another principal of Kwanzaa. *Imani* is the Swahili word for "faith." For centuries, loving parents have named their children Faith. And now, many black families are naming daughters Imani.

The Rev. Adam Clayton Powell, Jr., was a man of faith. As pastor of the prominent Abyssinian Baptist Church in Harlem, he served his community and looked out for the interests of all African Americans as a United States congressman for over two decades. During the turbulent 1960s he was known to say at the end of his activist sermons, speeches, and media appearances, "Keep the faith, Baby!" And of course, that caught on in the vernacular of popular culture language of the day. Now, in the new millennium, TV personality and author Tavis Smiley is the keeper of the "Keep the Faith" torch, closing his show every night with that same saying. It is at once holy and hip. Reverent and rap. A command and a prayer. Keep the faith. Do it!

REVERENCE

I feel that spiritual language is the way we really talk. Like Stevie Wonder's song says, "Just Have a Talk with God." When you're praying or talking to God you can communicate in any way you want. Keep the Faith, Baby! is as reverent as it is inspirational. One can be exuberant while being reverent. One can express humor while expressing honor. Whatever comes naturally that you know is from your heart is how you should express yourself.

If you don't use "thou" and "thine" in real life, don't worry about using them in prayer or when referring to God. Language evolves with the times. What doesn't change is human intention. If using "old English" makes you feel more reverent, that's fine too. But whether you use certain language or not, when you *feel* respectful—as though you are giving honor and adoration—you probably are respectful.

As an African American, I feel that I am not speaking in my "mother tongue" anyway. Poet Nikki Giovanni says that we don't speak English, we speak *through* it. It's our adopted language because we don't know the dialect of our original African tribe. There may be even more reverent ways to talk to God in our native language. How do I know that there aren't deeper, more worshipful words for expressing spirituality? I don't know, so all I can do is try to come to God with what I do know—the way I speak now. You know the hymn, "Just As I Am"? Well, God accepts us just as we are.

Aside from language, there are other ways to show our profound admiration for the sacred. When we take care of our bodies, we show reverence for them as our temples. When we attend religious services, or read sacred books, our actions express our spirituality. Each time we do these things we take our spirits higher, to an upper plane, and we get closer to our purpose.

I know a top corporate executive who pauses to give thanks for her food wherever she is eating. This person has the blessing of being able to dine in the best restaurants in the world, and at catered lunches at work. Whether it's a celebrity bash, business lunch, or takeout at her desk, she stops her conversation to go to a mental place of thanksgiving and reverence for the food her body is about to receive.

Each of us can create the space that feels natural to us to pause to acknowledge the spirit. It might be praying five times a day. It might be reciting a Buddhist chant. It might be a daily reading of a religious booklet. Wherever your spirit takes you is the way to reverence. Just take time to be holy.

GLORY

I read a book recently called *The Gospel of Good Success* by Kirbyjon H. Caldwell. The book's cover says it's "A Road Map to Spiritual, Emotional, and Financial Wholeness." I like how the author defines purpose as one's Calling. "I believe that a true Calling involves three different aspects: First the Calling glorifies God; second, it blesses, benefits, or helps somebody else; third, it brings you joy."

First, it glorifies God. If you believe that your mission in life glorifies God, how can you go wrong? That's a criteria that puts your purpose on a superb level from the beginning. If you start with that in mind, it's already a winner before you even create it.

How can you make your work glorify God? Let's look at some scenarios. Say you are a chambermaid that works in a hotel or an undertaker at a funeral home. You can look at your work as drudgery that pays the bills, or you can look at it as a service to people.

Here are some other scenarios:

Mission	*Gory Details*	*Glory Details*
Corrections officer	Works in jails with criminals	Helps someone toward rehabilitation
Hairstylist	Handles people's dirty hair	Transforms their crowning glory
Teacher	Has to discipline kids	Helps them reach their potential
Airplane pilot	Sees "air raged" passengers	Enables us to travel the world
Songwriter	Can write gangsta rap	Can have thousands singing praise

So you see, it is possible to totally ignore your high purpose and opt for the gory details of either failure or false success. But for every negative avenue, there's a positive one to travel. Just stop to think about how you can turn your mission inside out. In what ways can you give God glory? What is the ultimate way in which God can work through you? What can you do to benefit not only yourself, but others? Does your mission give you happiness, pleasure, satisfaction, and joy? If it doesn't, chances are it's not your mission. Keep on searching and you'll find the way to rise, shine, and give God glory.

One evening when I was tuned in to a television interview between Tavis Smiley and Denzel Washington, I heard Tavis take a spiritual departure from his conversation about the part luck plays in success to pay down-home homage to God—and to his grandmother: "Big Mama always said, 'There is no such thing as "good luck," but there is a good God.'" Amen.

JOY

Anita Baker sings "You Bring Me Joy." When I hear her sing, I have no doubt that she is following her purpose, and that it brings joy not only to her but to all who hear her.

Can you say that about what you think is your purpose in life? What satisfies your soul and makes your heart happy? Maybe you love storytelling, and you feel it is your purpose to tell stories of history or folktales to our children. Or perhaps you enjoy learning the technological aspects of computers, and feel it is your mission to help the world communicate easier. As Kirbyjon Caldwell stated, your purpose should bring you joy. It should reflect a burning desire that you translate into an inner light for others.

When you are following your purpose, you feel centered and balanced, clear and on point, alive and energized. Time goes by more quickly, leaving you wishing you had more hours in the day to devote to it. Even when you hit snags or frustrations, you never doubt that you are doing the right thing. In other words, your purpose brings you joy.

Carrying out our purpose through our joy is the common ground that all people can stand on. Two women, one black, the other white, had the same idea to spread joy. Suzanne Falter-Barns, who is white, wrote a book called *How Much Joy Can You Stand?* Her Web site, *www.howmuchjoy.com* sums it up right on the home page: "I figure what it all comes down to is faith. Have you got enough faith in yourself to make a break for it and run with your dreams? And do you have the courage to ask for, and get, the support you need? I invite you to begin the process right here, right now."

Then Suzanne gives us a checklist to start us thinking (reprinted here with her permission):

ARE YOUR DREAMS STARTING TO GET MOLDY?

Check those that apply to you:

____ There are things I want to do in life, and I'll get to them—when I'm in my nineties.

_____ If given a choice between devoting time to my business idea or rotating my tires, I'll go with the tires every time.

_____ I'd probably write the great American novel if I didn't have a television.

_____ I barely have time to feed my family, let alone my soul.

If you checked any of the above, read on . . .

Then the site provides a menu of choices to click on, including Inspirations, Joy Boards, Newsletter, Talks/Workshops, and more.

Debrena Jackson Gandy, who is African American, wrote a book called *All the Joy You Can Stand.* In it she says, "For most of us, joy has been so squeezed out of our lives, that we can tolerate it only in small doses. Or our joy thresholds are so low that experiencing joy in more than one area of our lives at a time can send us into "Tilt." We get so used to conflict, struggle, and hardship that we feel more at home "in strife" or struggling than we do "in joy."

"Thank goodness," she continues, "that we cannot overdose on joy. We are designed and 'wired' for it. . . . Besides, you deserve nothing less. Joy is your birthright. Joy is your nature. So let it in."

I like that phrase she uses: "in joy." We all need to spend more time in joy. We need to take time—and make time—to enjoy our selves, our children, our blessings.

How do we do that?

- *Experience the moment.* One of the most joyful moments of my life was spent lying in a hammock in Port Antonio, Jamaica. I was doing absolutely nothing. I thought to myself, *enjoy this moment of contentment. It won't last long—you'll have to get up eventually. But for now, just lie here and soak up the sun without a care in the world and feel blessed.*

- *Find joy in mundane things.* Opening your bills and finding a zero balance—that's joy. Fitting into a beloved garment you haven't been able to wear for years could qualify as joy, too.

- *Relive joyous occasions.* Pull out the video tape of your wedding. Tell your children stories of events they were too young to remember. Dust off your high school yearbook.

- *Know what brings you joy.* Does spending leisure time with your family make you happy? Does painting bring you joy? Do long week-end car trips make you feel carefree? Knowing what puts you "in joy" is the first step in going there. Think of it as a well of overflowing joy. Then try to find ways to drink from it as often as you can.

- *Keep a Joy Journal.* What makes you feel really good? I have no sta-tistics to bear this out, but I would wager that most people keep jour-nals to document their pain. By keeping track of our joy, we also keep the joy longer. We can return to it, and feel our delight once more. When we feel down or blue, we can try to counteract our feelings by reading about the good times.

BLESSINGS

As I mentioned, blessings are an important element of spirituality. Feel-ing gratitude for good fortune keeps us humble and grounded. From feeling the blessings of good health and happiness to experiencing the unconditional love of God and family, we can tap into our blessings and use them to reach our ultimacy.

For example, if you are a rich person, like say, Bill Gates, the co-founder of Microsoft, you can use your blessings of abundance to help others through philanthropy. That's obvious. But if you are more rich in spirit than in money, you can still share that blessing by giving of your-self. Blessed with a way with people? Volunteer your time at a shelter, food pantry, or senior citizen center. If you are a senior citizen who loves children, you can volunteer to become a Foster Grandparent at a hospi-tal, holding orphaned babies. Whatever your blessings, you can put them to work.

Sometimes we feel more stressed than blessed. But as we discussed in Chapter Three, there is good stress and bad stress. Planning your wedding is a good stressor. Moving to a new home can be good stress.

Bringing home a new baby is a source of blessed stress for many first-time moms. Keeping the stress in perspective can help to alleviate your sense of anxiety over it. Just as we say we are "stressed out" we can stake our claim to be "blessed out."

You are "blessed out" everytime you say, "Boy, that was fun!" Acknowledging and giving thanks for your safety and family and employment is being "blessed out." For some reason, cursing at someone is considered blessing someone out. But on the contrary, treating someone with kindness and compassion, courtesy and respect is more like it.

So many things we take for granted while we are distracted with our challenges are blessing us every day, every moment. It's just unfortunate that we don't often acknowledge them until we are in jeopardy of losing them. For example, if you are ill and bedridden, just getting out of bed in the morning would be tops on your "blessings radar."

Don't wait to have a problem to count those blessings. Name them one by one, day by day.

GIVING BACK

More sacred than counting your blessings is *being* a blessing. If your "cup runneth over," it is only natural—and spiritual—to have the desire to use the overflow to help someone else.

The concept of "giving back" indicates gratitude. It also conjures up images of putting something back into the community in the same loving way that it was given to you.

Even if you don't feel that you have a sense of abundance, giving back can make you feel better. Reaching out to help others by doing something that you love, can give you a feeling of accomplishment that is incomparable. When you help others, you help yourself.

Mentoring young people, volunteering with older folks, giving time at a shelter, running a clothing drive, collecting canned goods for a food drive, contributing to your alma mater, or organizing the community service project of your club—all these things and more are part of the underlying secret of spirituality that puts us on the path to our purpose.

We can give back, and we can also "give forward." That's what philanthropists call it when they exert control over the direction of their charitable giving. The average family gives 2.1 percent of their income, or an average of $750 a year. Wealthy people who can afford to give away at least $500,000 of their good fortune, commonly decide to start a private foundation, or a charitable gift fund. Whether you are rich in money, or mainly in spirit, whether you decide to give your time, or a monetary contribution, make sure you are doing it not out of duty but because of the spiritual benefit it can bring you. As the Bible says, it is more blessed to give than to receive.

God gives joyfully—and so should we.

PEACE

When you give back, it is common to have a sense of peace. Consider the following ways in which peace gives us power:

Inner peace is the type of tranquility we feel when our soul is at rest. When you know you have done your best, when you feel you have given your best effort, then you can experience inner peace. In difficult situations you may not always know what to do, but when you follow your intuition and handle things in a way that honors yourself, then you can feel inner peace. It's the payoff you get from knowing your own spirit and following it.

We live in times of iffy ethics and sometimey morals. It's often as easy to take home office supplies from your job for your child's homework or withhold information on your taxes as it is to do the right thing. But what you don't pay in money is deducted from your peace of mind. Telling the truth on your resume, being honest in your relationships, living life with integrity and dignity give you inner peace.

It takes some soul-searching to live with honor. And what gives you peace of mind may not be of any importance to those around you. That's because your inner world is unique to you. No one else can define it for you—and you can't define it for someone else. You can only mind your own mission, and leave other people's alone.

That is hard to do sometimes, because we all have such good intentions. We only tell others what to do because we think we know what is best for them. It is true that parents are meant to guide children in the right direction. However, we can't expect to live life for them. God has already made us, and we are already making our contribution to the world so we can't expect our children to be exactly like us. Now it is our children's turn to make mistakes and find their own way to what gives them inner peace.

We often feel that coming from a "dysfunctional family" contributes to our lack of inner peace. But we must also consider how our own dysfunction can interfere with the interior calm and quiet of others in our lives. Of course, cursing, fighting, harassing, loud-talking, talking back, gossiping, and backbiting are vexations to the spirit. But little things spoil the peace too. Do we play loud music when we know someone nearby is trying to study? Do we ridicule someone who takes time to meditate? Do we insist that friends accompany us to the mall when they would rather take a nap after a stressful work-week? If we increase the inner peace of others, we'll be better able to negotiate for them to do the same for us.

Domestic peace is the opposite of domestic violence. Besides war, domestic violence is one of the worst states in which to live. It is pure chaos of the spirit.

I know someone who grew up in a family in which the parents wed young, and were high-strung and volatile throughout the twenty-year marriage that ended in divorce. They fought hard and then they made up hard. There wasn't much difference between the noise level of the arguing and the abandon of the lovemaking. Neither bouts of passion contributed to the domestic peace of the household. This had an effect on my friend, who grew up determined to keep a peaceful home and who found role models in other family members from whom she learned how to disagree without being disagreeable. Her sister, however, grew up seeking peace at any cost. Unfortunately, that meant becoming a recluse. My friend is probably closest to the center, but you don't want to be either too volatile or too reclusive. Domestic peace is somewhere in between.

Keeping peace in your household is learning how to argue constructively. Using "I" sentences, like "I would like to have the sink clean when I go in the bathroom to wash up," rather than "You always keep that sink so damn nasty!" That may seem like an obvious example, but you'd be surprised how easily the situation and our attitude bring to mind that second scenario faster than the first. It gives us a false sense of power to sound like a "sister with an attitude." The edge in our voice masquerades for assertiveness, when in fact it is more likely a manifestation of either arrogance or insecurity. If you want a humble response, like, "Oh, I'm sorry, I'll wipe it off next time," you're more likely to get back what you give. It's common sense, but not common practice. Try it.

To live in our homes without fear but with a safety that is felt to the core of our souls is a blessing. Unfortunately, we don't always have control over the violent temperaments of others. No matter how nicely you conduct yourself, no matter how sweetly you use "I" messages, regardless of how disciplined you are, you just can't change some *other* people. If you are involved in an out-of-control domestic situation, please seek help. Call your local law enforcement agency if you feel you are in eminent danger.

World peace seems so lofty and out of our hands; on the contrary, we each play a part in creating and maintaining peace throughout the world.

I am old enough to remember the protests against the war in Vietnam. When I left home in Seattle, Washington, to go to college in Washington, D.C., it was during the height of the war. Protest marches were held with regularity on the mall between the Lincoln Memorial and the Washington Monument. Accustomed to participating in civil rights protests, I hadn't been active in the antiwar movement. But now that I was living in a dormitory only a few miles from the scene of major protests against a war in which I did not believe, I decided that I could not have inner peace unless I became involved. Unfortunately, I couldn't find many students to join me. Most black kids I knew drew the line down the middle: Blacks protested against racism, whites protested against the war. Both blacks and whites in each camp may have supported the others' efforts, but few crossed the lines to participate in the others' cause.

Martin Luther King, Jr., had crossed the line by speaking out against the war in the last months of his life, and some activists say he lost his life because of his views. Using him as a role model, I took the bus down Georgia Avenue and then walked over to the march alone. There was no police encounter or civil unrest, fortunately, and we all made our wishe known that we wanted peace in Vietnam by making a peaceful protest. "Peace" and "protest" are not mutually exclusive. I learned that day, that whether others join in your pursuit of what gives you peace of mind, you can follow your own heart. I can't say that mine became an important voice of opposition to the war after that, but I can say that my own pacifism was assertive that day, and it gave me peace. And maybe that meager effort helped to support the cause that eventually did bring the war to an end, as well.

Nonviolence was a tactic of the 1960s civil rights movement that King espoused after studying how Mahatma Gandhi used it in India. It has since been used worldwide, in 1989 at Tiananmen Square in China and at the May 2000, Million Mother March to protest gun violence here at home. Nonviolence is a tactic you can use in your own life, as well. Whether in a conflict in a remote part of the world or in a family-room dispute over the remote control, using the strategy that has been successful throughout the world is a first step toward increasing the peace.

Keep Gandhi's quote in mind: *Be* the change you want to see in the world.

Hope

When parents are arguing at home, when war is airing on CNN, when we read about gang violence in the newspaper, we hope it will stop.

Hope is our expectation of a positive outcome. It is what we cling to that keeps us from "losing it." With hope, our minds can anticipate a better day, an easier way of coping, an assurance and certitude in something greater than our current reality. Hope is spiritual thought.

We use hope in our most dire moments. When someone is close to death, we hope that person will live. In times of trouble, we hope and pray to find a way.

Ironically, we also hope to hit the Big Game $300 million lottery. ope we don't stand in line so long to buy the ticket that we'll bus home. Hope is with us daily.

ith, belief, and reverence, hope is an active word. It takes eyond what we experience for us to have it. We have to nourish hope, and nurture it to keep it alive, as Rev. Jesse Jackson, Sr., implores us to do.

In a spoof of Rev. Jackson's well-known call-and-response of "Keep hope alive!" comedians used to say, "Keep dope alive!" If you don't do dope or have a loved one addicted to it, that's funny. If you do, it can be dead serious. It just goes to show how close we all are from the flip side of our purpose. There may be times when you feel tempted to stray from our purpose, but hope and its accompanying spirituality can keep you grounded.

❧ The Secret Action Plan ❧

Whether temptation strikes or your spirituality just needs a pick-me-up, religion, prayer, meditation, and compassion are the ammunition we all have at our disposal to bolster our hope, belief, faith, and other elements of our spirituality.

PRAYER 1:1

It's the ultimate call when you feel small. It's the online connection to your purpose and protection. It's the satellite dish to your every wish. Nothing compares to prayer.

The concept of prayer may feel familiar to some of you, but have you ever put prayer into action?

- Prayer provides communication and communion with God: *I call on you, O God, for you will answer me; give ear to me and hear my prayer* (Psalms 17:6).

- Prayer is our soul's connection to its ultimate Source.

- Prayer helps us grow closer to God. No matter how old we are, we can always grow in spirit.

- Prayer allows us to give praise. "Allah u Akbar" or "God is Great" is one of the most common prayers in the world, expressed by Muslims and Christians.

- Prayer allows us to give thanks for God's blessings, power, glory, forgiveness, and mercy.

- In prayer, we can express the deepest desires of our heart, whether or not our mouths ever do. Singer Mary J. Blige once said about dreaming of her success, "Out of my mouth, I would say, 'Naw, it won't happen,' but in my heart I prayed it would."

- Prayer, which is ancient and primal, connects us to the universe and what is, what was, and what will be—God's will.

Praying for material things may not be the way to get what our spirit needs. Unity minister Phyllis E. Crichlow advises we make sure we've got our prayer request in order. "In the mid-eighties, with no job or car, I moved home to my mother's house in Palm Springs," she said in a sermon in March 2000. "In the church sanctuary, I prayed—begged—for a car, a job, a house. The Voice said, 'Seek ye first the kingdom of God, and all these things will be added to you.'"

Many of us pray as if we're talking to Santa Claus. We tell God to give us things. We ask God to deliver. We boss God around with commands of what we want Him/Her to do. Instead we should ask that God's divine will be done. When you are in need of prayer, or in a prayerful mode, Rev. Crichlow advises that we pray at least as much as you do other things. "Pray as often as you eat. Pray as often as you drink. Make prayer your most frequent activity next to breathing."

MEDITATION

Prayer is talking to God. Meditation is listening to God. In the stillness, we can hear the answers to our prayers.

Have you ever been around people who talk too much? I know folks who are a total vexation to the spirit because they yak, yak, yak, and rarely listen. Someone can be agreeing with them, but they are the last to know because they are too busy enjoying arguing their point. That's what happens to us when we have one-way conversations with God. We tell God what we think She should do, but we don't give Her a chance to be heard. In meditation, we can shut down, and say, "Okay, God, I sub-mit. I am listening."

My editor has a favorite card that reads, " 'God I've been praying and praying, but you haven't answered.' God replies, 'My child, I've answered many times, but you weren't listening.' "

Many of us shun silence. I am guilty, because the first thing I do when I come home and it's quiet, I turn on the TV. To meditate, or listen to our inner voice, we don't have to sit in a yoga position and look like a guru, although that would be an enlightened position to take. Those of us who are not ready, or don't think we have time for formal meditation, can begin by not slam-dunking the silences we encounter. Don't wear your Walkman to jog next time—listen to nature instead. Don't listen to your favorite DJ while getting dressed tomorrow morning; listen to the DJ of the Universe. Believe me, you just may hear a new song!

After you've successfully achieved a few moments of silence, in-crease the peace to twenty minutes a day, once a week. Then once a day. You may even crave more enlightenment and decide to sit in silence twice a day, morning and night, as my husband does. Turn off the TV, the phone, the radio, the Internet, to halt outside influences and get in touch with your inner voice. To block out visual distractions, pull down the shades and turn off the lights. But don't go to sleep. Use a timer or alarm clock if you need to avoid the silence and introspection.

If you would like to take your quest to the next level, learn more methods of meditation by taking a course or going to a spiritual retreat that gives immersion in meditation. Be ready to receive stronger mes-sages of spirituality than you've ever had before. Those messages may give you insight into your purpose.

That's what happened to Cynthia Badie, a New York City entrepre-neur, who says learning to meditate changed her life. "I meditate every day without fail now," Cynthia says. "It really centers me. When I med-itate I can focus on my mission."

It all started for Cynthia one day at the mall. "I saw that there was a Franklin Covey store, so I went and bought a Palm Pilot to get better or-ganized. In the store, there was a number to call for coaching on Stephen Covey's *Seven Habits of Highly Effective People*. I called and got the information, then signed up for the twenty-two weeks of Thursday assignments. Each week I call my coach and get my assignment. This week, for example, it's on procrastination. To carry out each assignment, I meditate each day. The coaching is also helping me to create my mission. So everything I do toward my mission in my day-to-day life is because it's embedded in my head."

Remember: Try self-meditation before self-medication.

RELIGION

If spirituality is a feeling of inner sacredness, then religion is organized spirituality. It's our choice and/or tradition of worship and praise that we hold holy.

Did you know that people who are more religious experience greater well-being? That's right, studies have shown that when we have religion in our lives, we experience more satisfaction with life, less anxiety, and less depression.

According to the Reuters news service, research suggests that people who attend religious services are healthier than those who do not and are less likely to smoke and/or drink excessive amounts of alcohol. In addition, strong social bonds such as those formed among congregation members may help boost immune system function, thus improving overall health.

One study published in the May 2000, issue of *Demography*, found that people who attend worship services one or more times each week generally live about eight years longer (to an average of age eighty-three) than those who never attend religious services (to about seventy-five). The latter had an 87 percent higher risk of dying from all causes during the nine-year follow-up period than those who attended services one or more times per week. The study further showed that the protective effects of attending religious services were strongest among women and blacks.

How does it work? Going to religious services increases social ties and influences other behavioral factors that keep us healthier longer and decreases the risks that bring on premature death. Just think of it—religious folks are more inclined to eat according to religious guidelines (like not eating pork), feel it is their religious duty to treat others kindly,

and hold beliefs grounded in hope and faith that keep them o
They may also feel it is counterreligious to smoke, drink alcoh
drugs.

Another study revealed differences in patients' health and pain
among those with high, moderate, and low levels of internalized spirituality. Those who said they were highly or moderately spiritual reported
better overall health and less physical pain than their counterparts who
reported low levels of spirituality. The Georgia Baptist Family Practice
Residency Program research team in Morrow, Georgia, led by Dr. J. Le-
Bron McBride, which conducted the study, even suggests that to help
with holistic treatment options doctors ask patients questions such as
"What does your spirituality mean to you?" and "How close do you feel
to a good or a higher power?," to give both doctor *and* patient an assess-
ment of the patient's spirituality.

You don't have to get sick to ask yourself those questions. The answers can give you a more holistic and holy life. And that can only
strengthen your purpose.

LOVE

Here are some things that have been written about love:

- Love is patient

- Love is kind

- It does not envy

- It does not boast

- It is not proud

- It is not rude

- It is not self-seeking

- It is not easily angered

- It keeps no record of wrongs

- Love does not delight in evil, but rejoices with the truth

- It always protects, always trusts, always hopes, always perseveres

- Love never fails

If this information sounds familiar it's because I got it from a very reliable source—the Bible (1 Corinthians 13:4–7).

Love is the most important element of spirituality. Jesus taught that we should " 'Love the Lord your God with all your heart and with all your soul and with all your mind.' This is the first and greatest commandment. And the second is like it: 'Love your neighbor as yourself.' " (Matthew 22:37–38)

One powerful way to show love for your neighbor, those who share the planet with you, is through *compassion*. A feeling of empathy for others, especially those who are suffering, distressed, or unhappy, compassion is a virtue that is sorely missing in the world today. In a society of more wealth and prosperity than in recent history, there seems to be less compassion. The wealthy have less compassion for poor people, resulting in a decrease in shared abundance and benevolence. Goodwill is not encouraged by popular culture that glorifies violence and arrogance. Fewer people are giving freely of themselves to the benefit of others.

My former sister-in-law, Susan Joy Anderson, who has always been a caring person and who has read the teachings of the Dalai Lama, calls compassion a "blame-free zone, a space to be nonjudgmental." When you approach strangers, neighbors, friends, relatives, and lovers with compassion, the result, Susan says, is a more peaceful world, more fairness, a better place.

In our love relationships, spirituality can serve as our guide in choosing a mate. I learned that the hard way after dating men who did not have much of an interior spiritual life. A couple had nice homes and flashy cars, but when I met Reggie, who drove a VW Bug, one of the things I admired about him most was his sense of compassion. Previously, I had dated a few guys who cared so much about themselves that they had nothing left to share with anyone else. Initially attracted to their smooth moves, I later found them to be cocky and egotistical, in the way that men who know they can—and do—attract a lot of women can be. But at the time I met Reggie, he was working at a foster-care home for boys as a counselor because, he said, "I heard that only women were working at the home, so the boys had no male role models. They needed a father figure in their lives." He knew his compassion made him the right person for that job, even though it didn't pay much and was hardly what one would call a power position that would land his picture in *Black Enterprise*. But for the two years, in his late twenties, that he worked there before pursuing his career as a sales executive, he was a positive advocate for those boys whose parents could not or would not raise them. Reggie was willing to give the boys attention and direction, and show them love and care.

Reggie was able to share his compassion, which gave his job purpose, because of his spirituality. As a young Muslim, barely twenty-three, he made the pilgrimage to Mecca, called *hajj*, in Saudi Arabia. Following in the footsteps of his hero, Malcolm X, he made his way from the States on this annual religious journey of the Islamic faithful. Several years later when we met, even though he and I were of different faiths, when he told me the story of his hajj and what it had meant to him and how it had had an impact on his life, I admired his devotion to God. Inspired by him, I hope to go to Israel, the Holy Land of my own Christian faith, someday. Throughout our twenty years of marriage I have also learned that when spirituality is the foundation of a person's own life, it makes for solid ground in a relationship filled with love.

In this chapter, I have said that without spirituality, a life of purpose is difficult to achieve. But I also want you to know that the reverse is also true: *With* the elements of spirituality, all things are possible. As the Bible says (1 Corinthians 13): *And now these three remain: faith, hope and love. But the greatest of these is love.*

💝 *Your Spirituality Journal* * 💝

How do you feel about your level of spirituality?

How is your life influenced by faith?

What things give you hope?

How are you giving love and compassion?

How do all of the above push you toward your purpose?

*Don't want to write in this book? Photocopy the page or use your own journal or notebook.

ℰSTEEM

Love yourself. Such simple words. Such a difficult task.

How can we love ourselves if the people closest to us have told us we are ugly, or dumb, or too black? Or if society has given us the message that only blondes have fun, or that you can never be too rich or too skinny—when you know good and well you'll never be blonde, rich, *or* skinny? And you know in your heart you shouldn't have to be because God made you what you are, and God doesn't make mistakes.

❧ What Is Esteem? ❧

"To regard highly and then prize accordingly," is how my electronic dictionary defines it. Esteem is the high regard in which we hold others and ourselves.

For all of us, self-esteem starts out on a high note. Do you know any babies with self-loathing? From childhood, however, as we learn about the world and our place in it, we develop an internalized set of core beliefs about ourselves. Repeated messages are unconsciously stored, always under the surface, forming how we feel about ourselves.

When self-esteem is low or nonexistent, it's usually because others have repeatedly told us negative things about ourselves, and we've believed them or we have used negative self-talk on ourselves.

Often we consider low self-esteem the domain of those with low incomes. But almost everyone has grappled with it at some point. Keeping self-esteem boosted in spite of the negative messages from others who have their own esteem problems is hard to do—but it can be done.

At the ten-year reunion of the Spelman College Class of 1990, one of the highlights was a forum called "Mind, Body, and Spirit." Those who participated were highly successful—as one would expect of alumni of this prestigious and competitive women's school in Atlanta. As one of the guest panelists, I noted that the group included physicians, airline executives, pharmaceutical marketers, and Internet entrepreneurs. Many who attended were married to equally successful men, and some lactating moms brought well-dressed, well-behaved infants with them to the event. Yet, as beautiful and privileged as these one hundred women were, when the doors to the auditorium closed and the conversation got real, the topic that dominated the discussion was how to hold on to your personal power.

"When I speak with college women," said panelist Dr. Beverly Guy-Sheftall, a distinguished Spelman grad and founding director of the college's Women's Research and Resource Center, "I find that they give their power away to men by doing such things as having sex without using condoms." This got an immediate response from the crowd. "I want to talk basics here with you today. Women need to learn to negotiate condom use. The threat of AIDS is real."

Guy-Sheftall's straight talk broke the ice and one woman asked urgently, "Just what is 'our power'? How do we define what that is?"

Panelist Patrice Gaines, a *Washington Post* reporter and author of *Laughing in the Dark: From Colored Girl to Woman of Color—A Journey from Prison to Power* tackled that one. "I think of our power as the essence of who we are, or all that we were when we were born. What I mean by this is that we enter this world with infinite power. We have this ability or potential simply because we exist. As we grow older, this potential to be whatever we chose, do whatever we want, is chipped away by people speaking negatively to us, by our own perception of what we can't do, or by negative images we have of ourselves. Once we realize what is happening and commit to rekindling our perfection, we begin the journey back to who we were in the beginning. In other words, we have to take back our power, or remember who we are."

In a personal conversation with Patrice later, she added, "I think of power as *all* that we are—this includes even the possibilities we don't realize or may never understand. I believe deeply that we as humans have only begun to scratch the surface of what it means to be human, so we perhaps may never really know the depths of our power. But we can allow it to flourish by having faith to simply believe it exists. And to honor our power by protecting and nourishing it."

In nurturing our self-esteem, we empower ourselves. We live with strength to do the things we know are best for our well-being, such as insisting on the use of condoms in our sexual relationships. When we feel empowered, we also relinquish the feelings of "desperation" that Dr. Guy-Sheftall says she sees among women who will do anything to have a man, and not be alone.

One of the alumnae took the mike to confess that she had suffered from bulimia when she was in college, and that a hospital stay that included intensive counseling had helped her. She bravely admitted that she could have felt shame and been reluctant to seek help, especially because she knew that word of her problem had gotten around campus and that people talked about her situation. "But what was more important," she said, "was that I got help." That, she added, is what she advised for any of her sister grads who might need it: seek counseling.

Other issues of esteem and self-empowerment came up at the forum, such as how to gain your strength and power following the loss of a parent. "When my mother died, I felt I had no one. I didn't know where to turn." Bereavement counseling was advised by Dr. Guy-Sheftall.

For Black women in particular, our mothers are often our backbone. Many of us were raised by women on whose strength and tenacity we relied. When society did not affirm us, our mothers did. So when that foundation is gone, we feel lost.

I am blessed to still have the strength, determination, affirmation, and love of my own mother. But having lost my father, upon whose wisdom and unconditional caring I also relied, I could understand where the sister was coming from. My response to her was that at some point we have to step up and "become our parents." As my father often said, "As they are, you will be." We can't stay "children" forever. We have to become the strong people that our mothers and fathers were for us; we have to do it for our own children.

If we think about it, who did our parents have to rely on when our grandparents passed away? Who gave them strength and faith? Where was the well of their self-esteem? How did they gather enough inner power to pass some along to us? When they were holding us up, who was holding them up?

Since the forum was on "mind, body, and *spirit,*" I felt free to say that the answer was God. When the earthly parent passes away, we are often guided to rely more fully on the ultimate parent, the parent of the universe.

If we have faith in God, it is easier to have faith in ourselves. If we believe in God, we can believe in ourselves and in the knowledge that the Spirit that moves in us can heal us, can keep us strong, can give us the confidence to hold on to our power.

When the Parent Is the Problem

Of course, not every mother or father is equipped to give us what we need to thrive and feel psychologically healthy. Many of them didn't get what they needed from *their* parents, so they don't know how to pass on anything better.

An elderly relative of mine was near death when she decided to forgive her stepmother for calling her stupid for years and saying that she'd never amount to anything. This person was very successful by anyone's measure and held in high esteem in the community, yet for almost her entire lifetime she had secretly defined herself by the emotional scars inflicted by the woman who had raised her after her own mother died when she was only two and her father remarried.

"You know," I said, trying to console her. "Not everyone has what it takes to raise us. Not everyone is prepared for our intelligence, especially if they suspect it surpasses their own. Your stepmother may have seen something that was so special in you that it intimidated her. Or maybe she was afraid your unbridled spirit would cause you harm, since you grew up during segregation. I'll bet she only said those things thinking she was doing the best she could. You are right to forgive her."

She looked at me and I could tell she was considering what I had said and that she was momentarily at a loss for words. But like any elder, she wasn't about to let me, the "young'un" think I had "schooled" her, so she quickly rebounded and deadpanned, "You've been looking at too much Oprah."

We laughed, but ironically there probably is more awareness within popular culture of the "issues" people face than there was when my relative way, say, in her early 30s. The stigma of getting help is slowly decreasing, and we have more signals from enlightened public people like Oprah, from magazines, and other media that it's okay to seek help in the form of counseling, therapy, group discussion, support groups, books, websites, and supportive friendships. That is progress.

As a matter of fact, I learned recently from a TV talk-show guest that fear is a way of expressing insecurity. If my relative's stepmother was intimidated by her own child, or was "afraid" of the ramifications of a black child's strong will, that "fear" was simply a feeling of insecurity about what the child would one day face.

As I mentioned before, we are all products of our own upbringing. As writer Toni Morrison said on *Oprah* in discussing her novel *The Bluest Eye,* which explores the effects of negative self-esteem, "Some adults are emotionally *thick.* You see the ravages of an unloved life."

If someone was not loved adequately in their own childhood, two things can happen when they have children themselves: they can treat them the way they were treated, or they can decide to treat their children in the way they would have liked to have been raised. Morrison advises, "Learn to treat your own children differently."

In addition, Morrison shared a rare glimpse into her own life. "As a parent, I could be what I wanted to be. People said to me, 'Aren't children confining?' But I felt that children just want us to have honesty, capability, humor, and the ability to deal in an emergency."

What our children require are virtues all society should value. If we could define ourselves by them, and not by those artificial values, we would be free to be ourselves, whether we are parents or not.

❦ *The Soul of Self-Esteem* ❦

To develop and maintain a healthy sense of self-esteem, writes Julia A. Boyd, a Seattle psychotherapist and author of *In the Company of My Sisters: Black Women and Self-Esteem,* "we need to receive two basic messages—'I am lovable, and I am worthwhile'—and we need to get these messages consistently. While these two messages seem fairly clear and direct, the reality is that they are very complex. The complexity is not in the words, but in our belief in the words. It's easy to say, 'I am lovable and worthwhile,' but much more difficult for us to believe it."

Boyd goes on to point out the three things it takes to turn a message into a belief:

1. The message must be given in a clear, direct manner.

2. There has to be supportive evidence that increases the validity of the message.

3. The message must be repeated over an extended period of time.

We may have desire for, but no control over, obtaining these messages from loved ones and others in our lives. But we can begin to take charge of sending ourselves these messages.

Research shows that changing your behavior can change how you see yourself and feel about yourself. See if there are any little changes below that you can try today:

• Open the door to self-love. Allow compliments to stick. Don't deflect them by countering with something negative. We've all done that: "What, this old dress looks nice? Girl, I've had this for ten years." Next time, try this: "Thank you! I enjoy wearing it."

• Find something to love the next time you look in the mirror. I have a big ol' mole right near the inside corner of my eye. I could hate it, but since I can't do anything about it, I decided to love it because it makes me look like me.

- Make a portfolio of images like yours. Cut out photos of women you relate to. If you are full-figured, look for *Mode* or *Belle,* publications that celebrate voluptuous women. Place the pages in plastic sleeves and a binder to make your own "magazine."

- Form a self-esteem team. Start a circle of folks with similar interests and support one another.

- Stop obsessing now! Quit looking at that same spot on your body that you detest every single day. Lock up your bathroom scale for a while.

- Leave. Get away from a person who doesn't affirm you. Do it for a minute (walk out of the room), do it for an hour (go to lunch), get away for a day (spend time with someone else), try for a weekend (visit your mama—unless she's the culprit!).

- Tell yourself "You're the greatest!" Muhammad Ali told the world why he thought he was the best fighter of all time. R. Kelly sang, "I Believe I Can Fly." Maya Angleou told everyone she was a "Phenomenal Woman." Write yourself a poem. Or at least make a list of all the ways you've got it going on.

- Make love with the lights on. Don't just look at your partner's luscious lips, either. Try to see what it is that he loves about loving you.

- Be gentle with yourself. You are a child of God. Treat yourself with the love and care you would give to someone sacred.

How? I've gathered some advice on self-esteem from some people who are held in pretty high esteem themselves.

🦋 Seven Secrets of Highly 🦋 Esteemed People

1. *"To succeed, get a sense of 'I AM,'"* said Dance Theatre of Harlem founder Arthur Mitchell, sitting ramrod straight in a television public service ad for Black History Month. He obviously has that sense of self, earned long ago, even before he had to cope with the pressure of being the first African American featured dancer with a major

American ballet company. "What Jackie Robinson was to baseball, I was to ballet," he said. "When you know who you are, you aren't afraid to let others know."

2. *"If you don't love yourself, you don't know what love is."* Rubin "Hurricane" Carter said this on Oprah's show when the movie based on his life was released. Can you imagine the low self-esteem he could have had after serving so many years in prison for a crime that he was later exonerated and released for? His secret for post-prison rehabilitation: "I started treating myself like I loved myself by sending myself four bouquets of flowers a week . . . No one can introduce you to your spirit but yourself."

3. *"Stand for something or you'll fall for anything,"* said R&B singer Bobby Womack on a BET Jazz Concert Special to explain why he refuses to curse in his songs, even when recording with Snoop Dogg.

4. *"Before you invest in your 'dream car,' the stock market, or that new relationship, take time to invest in your personal development,"* says self-esteem workshop leader Dianne Floyd Sutton, who is president of Sutton Enterprises in Washington, D.C. "This is one investment that no one else can make for you."

5. *"Every person has the same potential for inner tranquillity,"* stated the Dalai Lama at a lecture in New York's Central Park in 1999, "but 'negative forces,' such as fear, suspicion, selfishness, and self-hatred, can destroy inner peace."

6. *"I had to love and value myself more and stay true to what is important to me,"* writes Susan L. Taylor, publication director of Essence Communications, in her book *Lessons in Living.* "Spirit also revealed to me that I had already missed many opportunities for love because they hadn't come in pretty packages."

7. *"Don't take the negative comments of family members personally,"* advised a WNBC-TV commentator, discussing how to get along with family members on Thanksgiving. "They say more about them than about you."

BAD HAIR SCARE

Toni Morrison's *The Bluest Eye* shed light on how eye color and skin color affect African American self-esteem. A study conducted at Yale University found that anyone's self-esteem can plummet if his or her hair doesn't look "right." Advice columnist Ann Landers reported this, adding a personal comment, "For years, I thought if my hair didn't look the way I wanted it to look, I should wear a hat, put a scarf over my head, or stay home." In the Yale study, she continued, researchers questioned sixty men and sixty women, ages seventeen to thirty, most of them Yale students. Everyone in the study underwent basic psychological testing to determine their level of self-esteem. The conclusion was that those who were having a bad hair day had lower self-esteem than those who were not overly concerned about their hair.

Now, African Americans, who have long had hair issues that include the negative and pervasive terminology of "bad hair" and "good hair," could really take that study and conclude that if the general population feels that way about bad hair *days*, we must have rock-bottom self-esteem from bad hair *centuries*. Since our enslavement in this country, we have had to live with the stigma of having hair texture that is the total antithesis of the dominant culture's standard of beauty. To adjust our self-esteem, we have had to either alter our hair texture or alter our attitude about it. When we've attempted to try to fit in by changing the hair from kinky to bone straight, we have done so by methods such as burning hot combs or chemical "perms" that have often permanently damaged our hair, as well as our self-esteem. Just about every black woman I know has a "hair tale" to tell about the time her hair fell out, or her hairline was irreparably burned, or some other war story. It's like this sad sorority of women who have a "chemical dependence" on their hair relaxers—all because of the lack of esteem the world imposes on us when we allow our hair to be what it is.

I once had a conversation with a friend in her forties, who has a deep dark-brown beautiful complexion, about why she has never once worn her hair in its natural state. "I like it better this way," she said, referring to her perfectly coiffed bone-straight close-cut 'do, which has looked the same since she was a teenager. "But how do you know that if you've never even seen it any other way?" I asked. "Because I *know* this looks better on me." She began to get defensive and agitated, and refused to continue our conversation, so I backed off, knowing this was an issue for her. That was over ten years ago, and she is still wearing her hair the same way. I often wonder, *What is she afraid of?* What is the fear? What is the insecurity? Does she feel that she can't change the dark skin that has made her feel undervalued, but she can change her hair texture? Or is she afraid that the rejection her skin color too often engenders would only be compounded by the tight curl of her hair that goes along with it?

Whatever she feels, I can understand it. My own hair must have the tightest curl of the deepest Africa. But I decided to love it, since I couldn't really change it. I grew up in beauty shops with a standing every-other-Tuesday appointment for the hot comb. Yet no amount of straightening by the best hairdressers in my town could counter the spirit of my natural hair. No matter how well the hairdresser burned up the "kitchen," as we called the most resistant hair at the nape of our necks (which is probably how the texture came to be called "naps"), in a day or two, it would curl back up tight again. The "kitchen" always gave away the true texture.

Fortunately for me, I came of age in the "Black Is Beautiful" era. When Afros became chic, I was one of the first to embrace it at my high school. I decided that hair like that was special, that it was unique, that we should be happy that we are some of the few people God gave it to. I have had my hair hot-combed, relaxed, lyed, and dyed, but my soul is most at rest, I came to admit to myself, when it is in the natural state that God made it. It became a spiritual decision for me, and that raised my self-esteem. Who was I to change God's creation? No human had higher authority to decide that the way God made our hair was wrong.

I must say, though, that how black women feel about their hair texture seems to be how white women feel about their hair color. Does the old TV-ad question, "Do blondes have more fun?" really translate into "Will being a blonde give you higher self-esteem?" No one should be led to believe their self-worth is tied to being described as a blue-eyed blonde—unless you were born that way. But if you are negating your natural beauty, you are negating your best *self*—the place where purpose blooms. I have always admired the brunettes who didn't give in to the hype: Jacqueline Onassis, Audrey Hepburn, Elizabeth Taylor, Sophia Loren, Isabella Rosselini, Maria Shriver, Brooke Shields, Cindy Crawford, Christiane Amanpour, among others. And I'm sure anyone would agree these are women who also exude strong self-esteem.

BEST DRESSED OR BEST BLESSED?

At the Spelman forum, there was much debate over whether getting one's nails done, one's hair coiffed, and other self-pampering, contributed to self-esteem. One panelist admonished the audience, saying that women paid too much attention to the outer self and not enough on the inner person.

Then one sister took the mike to respond that getting her nails done was one of the few times in her week when she could escape her children and have time to herself. My own point of view was that if looking good makes you feel good then it is helpful (as long as it's not pinching your pocketbook), however, what is more important is what is going on in your head when you are out having those treatments. Do you allow yourself time to think when you are in the nail salon? Or are you gossiping? If you can't afford the dress you want, are you upset because you don't think you'll be best-dressed, or do you still consider yourself to one of the "best blessed"? If you do, you'll be "less stressed."

Fannie Lou Hamer was a woman whom Children's Defense Fund founder Marian Wright Edelman has described as a "great lady of the Mississippi civil rights movement, who lacked a college degree but certainly not intelligence or clear purpose." No one could have ever accused her of squandering money on designer clothes. She lived simply and humbly, yet she obviously had great inner strength that allowed her to challenge unjust laws that prevented blacks from voting in her state and take to task the entire Democratic Party at their national convention. There are some things that money just can't buy—self-esteem and the esteem bestowed upon you by others are two of them.

SELF-IMAGE: WHERE YOU COME IN

Outside forces over which we have little control can greatly, sometimes irreparably, erode our self-esteem. Incest, molestation, rape, and verbal or other abuse are life-changing tragedies that require patience, acknowledgment, and therapy in order for you to heal. I won't lie and tell you that I am an expert in those areas. But I do know that counseling is a first step toward that healing.

Over the everyday assaults on our feelings about ourselves, we can take some control. Try this quick quiz to see where you stand:

💟 *Are You Loving Your Body?* 💟

The question is not "Do you love your body?" to which you can easily say, "Sometimes." What we need is to be in a constant state of appreciation and care for our bodies. We need to be actively loving our magnificent, sacred machines. See how well you do, by answering "Yes" or "No" to the following ten questions.

1. Do you go for regular checkups during which you discuss your health and your weight with your physician?
   ___Yes, I get a checkup annually
   ___No, that's not something I do regularly

2. If you've gained weight over the years, do you dress for how you *used* to look?
   ___Yes, I still have the same style, even though it may not always be flattering
   ___No, I dress for my fuller figure

3. Are you more concerned with how you look than how you feel?
   ___Yes, if I look good, I know I've got it going on
   ___No, if I feel good, it helps me look good

4. Do you exercise regularly?

___Yes, I think it's more important to be toned than to be
skinny

___No, I'm too big to jump around in an exercise class

5. Is fitness fun?

___Yes, if I'm doing something I enjoy

___No, it's a pain in the neck no matter what the exercise

6. Do you diet frequently?

___Yes, whenever I need to lose some weight

___No, I know that gradual changes to lower-fat foods last
longer than fad diets

7. Do you like what you see when you look in the mirror?

___Yes, because I know my body is wondrous, no matter
what it looks like

___No, all I see are the same ol' flaws every time

8. Do you use language that degrades yourself?

___Yes, I admit that I never give myself any slack

___No, I am generally gentle when I talk to or about myself

9. Are you generous with compliments to others?

___Yes, I freely give a compliment whenever I feel it's due

___No, no one ever compliments me, so why should I
compliment anyone else?

10. Have you ever taken inventory of your friendships and
eliminated those that don't honor you?

___Yes, I have, and I do it with regularity

___No, I'm loyal to my friends, whether they are negative or
positive people

Answers: From the questions, you probably can guess the score: The
best answers are Yes to 1, 4, 5, 7, 9, 10; No to 2, 3, 6, 8. **8–10 best answers:** You have a healthy self-image. Keep up the good work! **5–7:** You
are headed in the right direction. Try harder to be more gentle with yourself. **4 and under:** Don't be so hard on yourself. Your body is an amazing
creation that no human can replicate—no matter what size or shape.

Here are some dos and don'ts related to each of those questions to consider:

1. **Do** get in the habit of scheduling annual regular check-ups. Don't just go to the OB-GYN. A general physical can give you the opportunity to discuss your overall health. In addition, if you feel you have a weight problem, your physician can advise you on just how much weight you need to lose and how to do it most effectively.

2. **Don't** make the mistake many women do of waiting until you have reached a desired weight before you buy new clothes. Invest in fashions that enhance the body type you have now, regardless of your weight. You'll feel better when you honor the body the way it is.

3. **Do** focus on how you feel. If you are a big woman, yet you feel energetic, full of stamina, and joy, then that is more important than what the scale says. That inner feeling will exude. Beauty does start within.

4. **Do** exercise regularly. You know the guideline: three times a week for at least 30 minutes a day; more often and longer if you are trying to lose weight. If you get in the habit of working out, you will begin to feel that you are taking control of your life, and that will boost your self-esteem.

5. **Don't** turn up your nose at fitness. If you work out doing an exercise you consider fun you'll be more likely to stick with it.

6. **Don't** say that four-letter word—diet. That is, unless you mean it as a lifestyle, as in "My diet consists of eating healthfully *all* the time." Banish the concept of *dieting*, that denotes a certain time period in which you plan to restrict yourself from the foods you love.

7. **Do** learn to appreciate your health, your shared family traits, your sight, a unique birthmark, and other features that make you who you are. What you see isn't all you get.

8. **Don't** talk about yourself like a dog, either. You know, the word "dog" is "god" backwards. Turn your language around.

9. **Don't** be stingy with your compliments. You give what you get. If you are sincere and liberal in expressing the genuine positive thoughts that come to you, you may not always get a return compliment, but you will acquire an inner spirit of generosity that won't cost a dime.

10. **Do** take inventory of your friendships. Are there any that don't honor you? Is every person deserving of a front-row seat in your life? Don't waste your time expending positive energy on people who only return negativity. Even if the constant bad vibes are not focused on you, it doesn't feed your self-esteem to hear constant bashing of someone else's. Put-downs of others do not raise us up. You don't need friends who only "Yes" you either, but if someone is truly "your girl," she's going to be supportive, caring, and compassionately honest with you.

A positive body image starts with a positive self-image. A cultivated self-image is one that is bolstered by enlightened self-esteem. And of course, everything I've said about being overweight can be applied to women who feel underweight as well. Feeling good about who you are is always more important than how you feel about how you look.

You can feel better about yourself if you consider that some people who look a certain way just *happen* to fit into a particular set of societal standards. The people didn't have to do anything but be born to acquire them, and the standards are artificial. Someone who looks "beautiful" among Americans may look totally ghastly among the Masai. Yet, there are virtues that are universal. Cultivating them can fortify you against the assaults of the artificial, yet pervasive messages of worth. Some of them include:

- Kindness
- Compassion
- Generosity
- Diplomacy
- Honesty
- Humor
- Graciousness

These are virtues that money does not guarantee you, that beauty does not bring. Living in the New York City area, I can't tell you how many times I have seen well-dressed, perfectly coiffed, and manicured women who look *sad*. The other day, I sat across the aisle on a bus from a most stylish Asian young woman. She had on an expensive pin-striped suit that was topped by a colorful Pashmina. Her impeccable public image included the latest shoes and bag, matching polish on hands and toes. She looked good enough to be photographed for *Vogue,* the building of which we happened to pass along the street this bus was traveling. But what struck me most was her expression—totally sad! She looked as if she hadn't smiled in *days*. I began to wonder what was going on behind the facade.

In contrast, I once worked at *Glamour* magazine with a young, spirited woman who was a joy to be around. She was pleasant to everyone and her sense of self-deprecation and fun made the hours, days, and years we worked together a happy memory. I really don't remember whether Cindy was a great dresser or not. I can't recall if she kept her nails polished or natural. But I recently opened *Harper's Bazaar* magazine and noticed that she is now the publisher—a position once reserved for men only. Cynthia Lewis's inner glow and strong sense of self had brought her outer success.

R-E-S-P-E-C-T

Perhaps one of the most important elements of esteem is that thing Aretha sang about. I'll bet that's why "Respect" was voted the #2 most popular roll and rock song on a cable music show I saw recently (what was #1? "Satisfaction" by the Rolling Stones). "All I ask is that you give me my 'propers' when you get home." Over 30 years later, young people are still asking for their "props"—proper recognition, proper acknowledgment, proper respect. It's what our spirit demands and what we have to give others.

Bob Law, a radio host on WLIB radio in New York City, is known for telling his listeners to "respect yourself." When listeners call in he tells them he respects them and they respond, "And I respect you." No one ever said, "Whenever you call into this show you have to say 'And I respect you.'" It just comes natural. When someone shows you respect, you feel obliged to give it in return.

Of course, Aretha was talking about a love relationship. And that is where we often take our cues of self-worth. Here are some thoughts on how to preserve your self-esteem in your intimate relationships.

❧ *Loving Without Drowning* ❧

Much of our self-esteem is tied into how we love and how loved we feel. Here are some thoughts on how to keep your inner power when you are in the most intimate of relationships—love.

Grow into love. If you think of "falling in love" like falling into a deep pool of water, you can understand that unless you know how to swim, you just may drown! Float first. Get to know a person, grow into a deep and meaningful relationship. Don't rush or force the bond. Just live in the present by enjoying each delicious moment you spend together.

Be true to yourself. It may sound cliché, but it's important. We are too often more true to someone we want to hold on to than we are to ourselves. We change our nature to make ourselves attractive. We try to be what we feel the other person will want, when we know that what is fake can't last.

I remember that I once had a boyfriend who was very athletic. He played tennis, so I took up tennis—spending gobs of money on lessons and court fees. He went skiing, so I hit the slopes—like a fool (since I couldn't even conquer the "bunny slope," reading a book at the lodge became my M.O.). He liked to backpack near camping areas, so I packed my suitcase and tried to "rough it" in a tent. None of this worked.

He could see right through me and ridiculed my every feeble effort at being a jock. Insensitive people who use you to build themselves up can always sniff out your weaknesses to go in for the kill. He enjoyed "teasing" me by calling me a wimp and a sissy, and I fell for it, feeling inadequate most of the time. Instead of berating myself, I should have seen that we were obviously mismatched. Time proved that to be the case. As Shakespeare said, "The truth will out."

You can only be who you are—and there's nothing wrong with that. Don't worry about finding the person who will appreciate your unique qualities. That divinely right person will appear when you are open to him or her. As one of my friends always says, "for every pot, there's a lid." I found my "lid" eventually, a man who accepts our differences—and so can you.

Don't define yourself by whether you are in a relationship. If you only feel worthy when you think somebody's in love with you, that's a dangerous place to be. It may seem like the top of the world, but if you hold yourself in high regard—taking care of yourself, loving who you are, pursuing your own dreams—all the time, whether you are in love or not, you'll be more likely to rebound "after the love has gone," as Earth, Wind, and Fire would say.

Love yourself foremost. You'll have more love to give if your giving comes from a well of self-love. If you care about yourself, you'll attract the caring of others. Many of us think we do love ourselves because of the many things we want for our lives. But what I am talking about is giving ourselves at least the same tenderness, the same patience, the same attention that we give to lovers.

It is a tall order for any person to be expected to make another person feel validated. Would you want that kind of pressure? I wouldn't. It's one thing to be a loving, supportive partner, but quite another to be expected to fulfill someone's needs for self-affirmation. That's the kind of neediness that can pull a relationship apart.

No one can *give* someone else self-esteem. It's something each of us has to develop for ourselves, and keep working on—with or without a partner.

Keep your own pursuits. When you fall for a new man, do you abandon your past life and make him your whole life? Do your friends stop seeing you? I know so many women who drop out of sight once they start dating someone. Heck, I've been one of those women myself. Before I met my husband, I was getting my exercise groove on, taking weekly modern-dance lessons at Alvin Ailey, but as soon as we started dating—that was the end of that! I was busy being preoccupied.

But guys rarely do that. Sitting home *alone* (after all your sister-friends have gotten tired of you saying no, so they've stopped asking you to the book-club meetings or the girls' nights out), you're wondering why your honey hasn't stopped hanging with the fellas on Thursday nights, or playing basketball every Saturday morning. Instead of taking it personally, interpreting it that he doesn't care about you enough to stop hanging with his male friends, take it as a tip: continue to be the person you always were. You'll feel better about yourself, and you'll stop obsessing about what he's doing when you are doing something that makes you happy, as well.

Be a friend. It's dangerous to think that love and friendship do not mix. In my personal survey of relationships that I admire, I see a firm foundation based in nonsexual common ground.

A young friend of mine was telling me how hurt she was that the man she had been dating said he wanted her to be a friend. She took this as a rejection, because she felt that once they had made love that meant that they were no longer friends, but were now "lovers." In reaction to his desire for love *and* friendship, she broke up with him. But I told her that I felt she shouldn't have been offended. Passion, lust, and romance are wonderful and heady, but hard to maintain day to day. If she was hoping to eventually marry him she would need to think about the ingredients of a longterm relationship. The secret of holding it all together during those non-sexy times of bill-paying, childrearing, and career building is companionship and devotion that is akin to the kind of relationship you have with long-time friends. After you mix those ingredients together, the icing on the cake is that you get to be lovers too.

Form a partnership. If you can be friends, you can be partners. In a love relationship where there is a partnership, there is no one with the balance of power. There is no dominating, abusive spouse; there's no belittled "little woman." When two whole people come together, a whole relationship can emerge.

Each of us brings our own strengths and weaknesses to our relationships. When we accept those characteristics in our partner, we can create an equal partnership that builds on our differences and commonalities. For example, if you were a math whiz in school, yet your man can hardly be bothered with balancing his checkbook, why should he be expected to handle your finances? If you volunteer to do the family math, you won't be arguing so much about money—and your self-esteem will be bolstered by your leading role.

Bend gender roles. Speaking of roles, hey, it's the new millennium. We just can't be tied to those antiquated rules about what men must do to take care of women, and what women have to do to be considered feminine. In black families, for example, women have always been on the vanguard of working outside the home, having had a history of it. And more recently, a study reported in *Heart & Soul* found that black fathers are more nurturing than white dads. "Black fathers seem to be gentle and warm with both girls and boys," explains study coauthor Ziarat Hossain, Ph.D., of Fort Lewis College in Durango, Colorado, "That may mean that black fathers are equally accepting of sons and daughters and may have similar expectations of them." That is certainly good news for the self-esteem of our children. When we encourage men to show their nurturing side and step aside enough to allow them to take leadership in care-giving, we stand a better chance of sharing those duties. And all that strengthens us.

Look for relationships to complement you—not complete you. Like your mother probably said, no one can take better care of you than you can take care of yourself. You are not a child who needs to be "taken care of" anyway—that sounds so co-dependent and immature. You are "all woman." And like any independent adult, you are open to love, respect, and companionship.

We are born complete and whole. Our love relationships should only enhance us and embrace who we are and what we hope to become. That alone would be a beautiful thing.

Whether we are in or out of love, esteem is the steam of our purpose in this life. Giving back to the community, helping others less fortunate, caring about what happens in other parts of the world, giving time and money to charitable causes, all help us to come out of our shell and be people of purpose in this world. Love others and we will be loved. Show others they are worthwhile, and we will recognize that feeling when it comes back to us.

❦ Be Who You Are ❦

As Arthur Mitchell says, we need to develop a sense of "I am" that will help us to live in the present, rather than in the midst of past wounds and hurts. Keep affirming who you are, who you were meant to be, and who you want to be, with daily affirmations, positive messages posted on your bulletin board or office cubicle, reassuring journal entries, and like-minded friends.

The reward for nurturing your self-esteem is endless abundance of freedom, wholeness, harmony, tranquillity, confidence, security—all of which overflows into caring, generosity, real love and esteem for others. When you achieve these things, you will find yourself in a constant state of minding your mission.

💜 *Your Esteem Journal* * 💜

What song exemplifies how you feel about yourself?

What is your favorite poem or quote with a positive message of esteem?

List a key to esteem that you already hold.

What area of self-esteem do you need to work on?

Reaffirm your purpose: "I feel it is my purpose to . . ."

*Feel free to write in this book if it's yours. Otherwise, make a photocopy of this page or use your own journal.

God put you here on earth on purpose
and for a purpose:
to uniquely manifest love.
Knowing, accepting, and living that fact
is the ultimate soulful secret.

PERMISSIONS

The author gratefully acknowledges the following:

Debrena Jackson Gandy, author of *All the Joy You Can Stand:
101 Sacred Power Principles for Making Joy Real in Your Life*
(Crown Publishers) for permission to quote a portion of her
book. Log on to her Web site at *www.debrenasworld.com*.

Suzanne Falter-Burns for permission to quote from her Web
site, *www.howmuchjoy.com* and her book *How Much Joy Can
You Stand?* (Ballantine Wellspring).

"Amends to the African-Americans" from *Illuminata: A Return
to Prayer* by Marianne Williamson, Copyright © 1994 by
Marianne Williamson. Reprinted with permission of Random
House, Inc.

"I Believe" words and music by Ervin Drake, Irvin Graham,
Jimmy Shirl, and Al Stillman. TRO—© Copyright 1952
(Renewed), 1953 (Renewed); Hampshire House Publishing
Corp., New York, NY. Used by permission.

Organon Inc., West Orange, NJ, for permission to reprint
from their "Women's Health" poster. For more information,

visit their Web sites, *www.organoninc.com* and
www.organonwomenshealth.com.

The Star-Ledger of Newark, New Jersey, for their series on the
Seton Hall University fire: "Her Sacrifice Set Seton Fire
Victim Apart," by Meg Nugent, February 4, 2000, News
Section, page 1.

THANK-YOU NOTES

The number-one soulful secret of writing a book is to allow purposeful people to surround you with their positive vibes. I gratefully thank those who did.

The Oliver Girls
Anique, Amena, Aleeyah, Ahmondyllah

The Family
Joyce Oliver, Arthur Braithwaite, King Ashford, Vicki S. Stokes, André S. Wooten, Daphne Barbee-Wooten, Gloria Leonard, Melanie Smith, James Leonard, Tina Brown, Lisa Brown, Alexis Anderson Wooten, Susan Anderson, Jill Hayott, Keith Copeland, Ronald Oliver, Muhammad Oliver, Syble Oliver, Bahia Oliver Mayes, Wesley Copeland

My Agent
Victoria Sanders

My Editor
Janet Hill
Her assistant, Roberta Spivak

My Publishing Attorney
Gizelle Galang

Research Associate
Tracy E. Hopkins

Purposeful People Who Shared Their Stories for This Book
Marianne Williamson, Rev. Phyllis Crichlow, Dr. Karen Dias-Martin,
Marie Brown, Michelle Burford, Debrena Jackson Gandy, Cynthia
Badie, Jacqueline Moody, Caryl R. Lucas

Sister-Friends
Erlene Wilson, Marlene F. Watson, Shelia Baynes, Audrey Edwards,
Brenda Yearwood Stone, Helena Mitchell Lindsey, Valerie Wilson
Wesley, Susan L. Taylor, Benilde Little, Iqua Colson, Ethelyn Bowers,
Winona Hauge, Michele Rawls, Gail Kendrick, Wendy Rountree,
Olivia G. Shaw, Nina Wells, Susan Long Walsh, Geraldine Smith-
Thomas, Patricia Ramsay, Marlene Kahan, Adunni Anderson,
Harriette Cole, Victoria Pinderhughes, Patricia A. Johnson, Leslie
Williams

The "Brown Angels" at NiaOnline
Cheryl Mayberry, Bonita Coleman, Darcy Prather, Linda Villarosa,
Teresa Ridley

Angels Who Art in Heaven
Daddy, Gran, Aunt Katie, Aunt Pat

Every Reader of This Book
You

ABOUT THE AUTHOR

Stephanie Stokes Oliver is vice president and editor-in-chief of NiaOnline, an Internet community of information and inspiration for African American women. In 1994, she helped to launch *Heart & Soul* magazine as its first editor-in-chief, after serving many years as the editor of *Essence.* Oliver started her career as an editor at *Glamour,* upon graduating with honors in journalism from Howard University. She is the author of *Daily Cornbread: 365 Secrets for a Healthy Mind, Body, and Spirit;* has written for *O: The Oprah Magazine* and *Good Housekeeping,* among other publications; and is a frequent public speaker. A native of Seattle, Oliver now lives in Montclair, New Jersey. This is her second book.